Devil's Advocates

DEVIL'S ADVOCATES is a series of books devoted to exploring the classics of horror cinema. Contributors to the series come from the fields of teaching, academia, journalism and fiction, but all have one thing in common: a passion for the horror film and a desire to share it with the widest possible audience.

'The admirable Devil's Advocates series is not only essential – and fun – reading for the serious horror fan but should be set texts on any genre course.'
Dr Ian Hunter, Reader in Film Studies, De Montfort University, Leicester

'Auteur Publishing's new Devil's Advocates critiques on individual titles... offer bracingly fresh perspectives from passionate writers. The series will perfectly complement the BFI archive volumes.' **Christopher Fowler,** *Independent on Sunday*

'Devil's Advocates has proven itself more than capable of producing impassioned, intelligent analyses of genre cinema... quickly becoming the go-to guys for intelligent, easily digestible film criticism.' ***Horror Talk.com***

'Auteur Publishing continue the good work of giving serious critical attention to significant horror films.' ***Black Static***

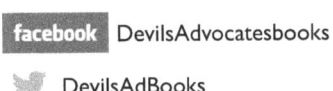

facebook DevilsAdvocatesbooks

DevilsAdBooks

ALSO AVAILABLE IN THIS SERIES

A Girl Walks Home Alone at Night Farshid Kazemi

Black Sunday Martyn Conterio

The Blair Witch Project Peter Turner

Blood and Black Lace Roberto Curti

The Blood on Satan's Claw David Evans-Powell

Candyman Jon Towlson

Cannibal Holocaust Calum Waddell

Carrie Neil Mitchell

The Company of Wolves James Gracey

The Conjuring Kevin J. Wetmore, Jr.

Creepshow Simon Brown

Cruising Eugenio Ercolani & Marcus Stiglegger

The Curse of Frankenstein Marcus K. Harmes

Daughters of Darkness Kat Ellinger

Dead of Night Jez Conolly & David Bates

The Descent James Marriot

The Devils Darren Arnold

Don't Look Now Jessica Gildersleeve

The Fly Emma Westwood

Frenzy Ian Cooper

Halloween Murray Leeder

House of Usher Evert Jan van Leeuwen

In the Mouth of Madness Michael Blyth

It Follows Joshua Grimm

Ju-on The Grudge Marisa Hayes

Let the Right One In Anne Billson

M Samm Deighan

Macbeth Rebekah Owens

The Mummy Doris V. Sutherland

Nosferatu Cristina Massaccesi

Peeping Tom Kiri Bloom Walden

Repulsion Jeremy Carr

Trouble Every Day Kate Robertson

Saw Benjamin Poole

Scream Steven West

The Shining Laura Mee

Shivers Luke Aspell

The Silence of the Lambs Barry Forshaw

Suspiria Alexandra Heller-Nicholas

The Texas Chain Saw Massacre James Rose

The Thing Jez Conolly

Twin Peaks: Fire Walk With Me Lindsay Hallam

The Witch Brandon Grafius

Witchfinder General Ian Cooper

FORTHCOMING

[REC] Jim Harper

Re-Animator Eddie Falvey

Devil's Advocates

The Evil Dead

Lloyd Haynes

Acknowledgements

Special thanks to Neil Casanova and Jane Giles for their invaluable assistance, Rob McLaine for permission to use the *Book Of The Dead* interviews, and to Bill Warren, who got there before me.

First published in 2021 by
Auteur, an imprint of
Liverpool University Press
4 Cambridge Street
Liverpool
L69 7ZU

Series design: Nikki Hamlett at Cassels Design
Set by Cassels Design

All rights reserved. No part of this publication may be reproduced in any material form (including photocopying or storing in any medium by electronic means and whether or not transiently or incidentally to some other use of this publication) without the permission of the copyright owner.

British Library Cataloguing-in-Publication Data
A catalogue record for this book is available from the British Library
Stills from *The Evil Dead* © Renaissance Pictures.

ISBN paperback: 978-1-80085-935-7
ISBN hardback: 978-1-80085-934-0
ISBN epub: 978-1-80085-812-1
ISBN PDF: 978-1-80085-852-7

Contents

Introduction 7

Chapter 1: Within the Woods 11

Chapter 2: The Ultimate Experience in Gruelling Terror 27

Chapter 3: The 'Bad Dream' and the 'Bad Place' in *The Evil Dead* 43

Chapter 4: Ash as the 'Final Girl' 61

Chapter 5: 'The Number One Nasty' 71

Chapter 6: The Influence and Legacy of *The Evil Dead* 91

Bibliography 111

INTRODUCTION

One of the most inventive and dynamic horror films of the last 40 years, Sam Raimi's debut feature *The Evil Dead* (1981) transcends its modest budget and limited resources by embarking on a turbulent and phantasmagorical journey into a gore-soaked hell. Released during a period when the slasher film cycle – commercially acceptable thanks to John Carpenter's *Halloween* (1978) and Sean S. Cunningham's *Friday the 13th* (1980) – had blunted the genre of much of its creative edge, *The Evil Dead* emerged like a thunderbolt, a surreal, absurd assault upon the senses.

This book is less concerned with the sequels, remakes and derivatives (although they will be considered in Chapter 6), rather it serves as an introduction to *The Evil Dead* itself and the territory it inhabits. Many still prefer Raimi's first sequel, *Evil Dead II* (1987), a bigger-budgeted, gleefully outrageous exercise in black humour and flesh-crawling horror, but the original is undoubtedly sturdy enough to stand on its own and be acknowledged as a genre classic.

The primary aim of this book, then, is to attempt to reinforce that position by asking just what it is that makes the film function as well as it does. Is it simply the overwhelming enthusiasm of the novice filmmakers? Is there some inherent quality in the script, direction or cinematography which allows it to soar majestically far above the dank Tennessee woods where the movie was shot?

There really wasn't another horror film quite like *The Evil Dead* in the early 1980s, and this book will seek to understand why.

SYNOPSIS

Ash, his girlfriend Linda and sister Cheryl and their friends Scott and Shelly decide to spend the weekend together in an isolated Tennessean mountain cabin. To reach their destination they must drive across a rickety wooden bridge, chunks of which fall into the river below. Although one of the wheels briefly becomes jammed in one of the rotten planks they pass safely to the other side.

Arriving at the cabin in the late afternoon, Scott unlocks the door and examines the dusty interior. Later, while alone at the window in one of the rooms, Cheryl is sketching the clock on the cabin wall when, precipitated by the chiming of the clock and a gust of wind, she finds herself inexplicably unable to control the pencil in her hand. Her attention is then drawn to the cellar trapdoor, which begins to push itself upwards for a few moments before calm is restored.

Some time after, as the group are having dinner, the trapdoor suddenly flings itself open. Scott descends the cellar steps to investigate and Ash hesitatingly follows. Amongst the bric-a-brac they discover down below is a shotgun, a large skull-hilted dagger, and an unusual book with what appears to be a face carved into the cover. Although the book's text and illustrations are indecipherable, Ash comes across a tape recorder which he then takes upstairs for the group to listen to. The voice they hear on the tape explains the following:

> It has been a number of years since I began excavating the ruins of Kandar with a group of my colleagues. Now, my wife and I have retreated to a small cabin in the solitude of these mountains. Here, I continued my research undisturbed by the myriad distractions of modern civilisation, and far from the groves of academe. I believe I have made a significant find in the Kandarian ruins. A volume of ancient Sumerian burial practices and funerary incantations. It is entitled 'Noturan Demonto', roughly translated, 'Book of the Dead'. The Book is bound in human flesh and inked in human blood. It deals with demons, demon resurrection and those forces which roam the forests and dark bowers of man's domain. The first few pages warn that these enduring creatures may lie dormant, but are never truly dead. They may be recalled to active life with the incantations presented in this Book. It is through recitation of these passages that the demons are given license to possess the living.

Cheryl switches off the tape recorder but Scott turns it on again, fast forwards and then plays a section in which the voice is reciting ancient sounds, which could possibly be the incantations from the book. Outside the cabin a mist begins to shroud the trees and the earth splits to reveal a blazing red light beneath the surface. Cheryl screams at the others to turn off the tape as a tree branch breaks one of the windows.

Ash offers Linda a silver necklace as a gift while an unseen presence observes them from outside. Sensing that there may be someone looking into her bedroom window,

Cheryl ventures into the woods, calling out to whoever is lurking there. The presence, or Force, unleashes a multitude of vines which wrap themselves around Cheryl's wrists, neck and ankles, tear away her bathrobe and proceed to sexually assault her. She succeeds in breaking free and runs through the woods, pursued by the Force.

Ash helps her inside as she fumbles to unlock the cabin door. Hysterical, Cheryl insists on leaving and her brother agrees to drive her into town, but the bridge they crossed earlier that day is now completely destroyed. After they return to the cabin Ash listens to more of the tape recording:

> I know now that my wife has become host to a Kandarian demon. I fear that the only way to stop those possessed by the spirits of the Book is through the act of bodily dismemberment. I would leave now to avoid this horror, but for myself I have seen the dark shadows moving in the woods, and I have no doubt that whatever I have resurrected through this Book is sure to come calling for me.

Linda and Shelly play a game where they attempt to guess the playing card they are holding; when Cheryl, sitting at the window with her back to the others, correctly announces each card she turns suddenly to reveal a demonic visage and cackling, witch-like voice. She begins to levitate before dropping to the floor, seemingly unconscious. As Ash approaches her, Cheryl, in the full throes of a demonic possession, jerks awake and stabs a pencil into Linda's ankle and hurls both her and Ash against the wall. Scott succeeds in kicking her down into the cellar, hastily securing the trapdoor.

The Force breaks through the bedroom window and advances towards Shelly. Her boyfriend races into the room after hearing her scream and she suddenly attacks him. Scott uses his knife to slice into the now-possessed Shelly's hand as she attempts to stab him with the ornate dagger but she manages to chew off the bloody limb. With her severed hand still attached to the hilt, Scott plunges the dagger into her back before dismembering her with an axe. Ash and Scott bury the twitching remains of Scott's girlfriend in the woods, while inside the cabin Linda is transformed into a demon.

With Scott grievously wounded, Ash is taunted by the possessed Cheryl and Linda, who then trick him by appearing normal and cured. Returning to her possessed state, Linda is stabbed by Ash, who chains her to a bench in the tool shed but is unable to bring himself to use the chainsaw he has revved up to dismember her body, deciding instead to bury her next to Shelly; when she rises up once again Ash decapitates her.

Returning to the cabin he discovers that Cheryl has broken out of the cellar; she continues to attack him even after he's blasted her with a shotgun. Having run out of shells he ventures back down to the cellar, where the overhead pipes crack open and spray blood across the walls, lightbulbs fill up with the stuff and a gramophone and cine-projector suddenly develop a life of their own.

Upstairs, Scott is reanimated as a demon and launches himself upon Ash. Now assaulted by two demons, the blood-drenched Ash succeeds is throwing the offending Book of the Dead onto the log fire. Cheryl and Scott, together with the terrible face which decorates the Book's cover, proceed to writhe, decay and ooze gallons of brightly coloured gunge.

As dawn breaks over the forest, an exhausted Ash emerges from the cabin, only for the Force to rush towards him with frightening velocity. The film ends as he turns and screams towards 'It'.

Chapter 1: Within the Woods

Born in Royal Oak, Michigan, on 23rd October 1959, Sam Raimi's formative years appear, in hindsight, to be one long, exhaustive preparation for what would become his first feature-length movie, *The Evil Dead*. Interestingly, given Raimi's subsequent close association with the genre, the horror film did not appear on his radar until 1978, and the experimental decision to direct the Super-8 short *Within the Woods* (1979).

Raimi was influenced first and foremost by zany, slapstick comedy in the style of the American vaudevillian, film and (later) television trio the Three Stooges, who were immensely popular from the 1930s through to the 1950s (the Stooges' influence would stretch across to *The Evil Dead* and, most significantly, *Evil Dead II*). Between 1972 and 1979 Raimi, in repeated collaboration with actor Bruce Campbell (b. 22nd June 1958) and co-director / actor Scott Spiegel (b. 24th December 1957), directed a total of 17 short Super-8 films, some at his parents' home in Michigan as a goof, others while studying at high school (Wylie E. Groves in Birmingham, Michigan) and at various summer theatrical gatherings.[1]

Josh Becker (b. 17th August 1958),[2] another key member of this small repertory company, describes the processes behind the making of the Super-8 shorts:

> Scott started making movies the earliest doing Three Stooges remakes, which used the actual soundtracks from the Stooges' shorts to which Scott and his fellow Stooge impersonators lip-synched. Sam and Scott became a team for a while making original short films that were all slapstick comedies. This is when Bruce stepped up and became the leading man. I'm pretty sure there were no scripts, shot lists or storyboards for any of these films, although Sam and Scott clearly knew what they were going to shoot ahead of time and were prepared with lines and props and costumes when the time came. My films, on the other hand, all co-produced with Bruce, had scripts, storyboards, prop lists, etc. These films were of a more eclectic nature, ranging from comedy to drama to suspense to action. By the end of the Super-8 era, and including a few 16mm shorts, Scott and I had teamed up to make slapstick comedies, with Bruce and Sam's help, and Sam had switched to horror, with Bruce, Scott and Rob Tapert's assistance. (Becker, 2019, online)

Spiegel would remake one of these films, *Night Crew*, in 1988 as *Intruder*, co-produced by Lawrence Bender (Quentin Tarantino's producer on *Reservoir Dogs*, 1991), the film features Raimi, his brother Ted and Campbell in small acting roles, along with Spiegel himself and special make-up effects maestro Gregory Nicotero (*Evil Dead II*). In 1985 Becker transformed another early effort, *Stryker's War*, into *Thou Shalt Not Kill... Except*, which was produced and co-written by Spiegel and featured micro-cameos from old friends Campbell and Sam and Ted Raimi.

Rob Tapert (b. 14th May 1955) was another Michigan native and compatriot of Sam's elder brother Ivan (an occasional actor who co-wrote the third instalment in the *Evil Dead* series, *Army of Darkness*, 1992) at Michigan State University, where he studied economics. Finding himself attracted to the frolicsome films which Raimi, Campbell and Spiegel were turning out in rapid succession during the mid-to-late 1970s, he suggested to Raimi that a shift from comedy to horror might be beneficial, both creatively and (hopefully) commercially.

THERE WILL BE BLOOD

> At the time, horror films scared me and I didn't like being scared. It was an unpleasant experience for me. But since making my first horror film, I've come to appreciate them, and to appreciate the great artistry of the classics. (Raimi in Warren 2000: 33)

In the autumn of 1978 the seeds were sown for what would become Sam Raimi's definitive Super-8 project, *Within the Woods*. Rob Tapert recalls himself and Raimi attending an early screening of John Carpenter's *Halloween*:

> Sam and I went to see it alone, and we were about the only people in the theatre, on a Tuesday night after it first opened in Lansing. Because we were alone, I didn't have a wild visceral reaction. I had seen a lot of drive-in movies because I liked them. I thought, 'Oh, this is pretty cool, and it's not the same as Hammer horror'. I asked him, 'Sam can you make a movie this good, maybe better than this?' He said he didn't know, because it was pretty good. I started doing research, found *Variety* for the first time, went back and got all their rental champs, and started pulling a bunch of stuff together. Eventually, I came up with information that was encouraging; some of the

biggest low-budget hits had been horror movies: *Night of the Living Dead*, *The Last House on the Left*, *The Texas Chainsaw Massacre*. And a lot of them had first-time directors. (Tapert in Warren 2000: 33-34)

Fig. 1 Tobe Hooper's The Texas Chainsaw Massacre.

Fig. 2 Wes Craven's The Hills Have Eyes.

The next step was convincing the likes of Bruce Campbell and Scott Spiegel that horror could be as viable an option as comedy; the others quickly agreed. As with so many novice filmmakers before them, the eager troupe understood – as Tapert's research had proven – that most of the commercially successful American horror movies released in the previous decade had been written and directed by young men like themselves with little or no experience beyond student shorts and advertising spots. Rob Tapert tendered the initial ideas for *Within the Woods* by identifying three primary sources of cinematic inspiration: George A. Romero's *Night of the Living Dead* (1968), Tobe Hooper's *The Texas Chainsaw Massacre* (1974) and Wes Craven's *The Hills Have Eyes* (1977). It's worth noting here the interesting production and distribution history of a movie which Kim Newman has described as 'the first horror film to be overtly subversive' (Newman 1988/2011: 16).

NIGHT OF THE LIVING DEAD

The terrors of George Romero's groundbreaking debut are immediate and contemporary, reflecting a 1960s America which is coming apart at every nail. Inspired by Richard Matheson's outstanding 1954 novella *I Am Legend*, about the last human survivor of an apocalyptic plague which has ravaged civilisation, as well as EC Comics, Edward L. Cahn's 1959 low-budget science fiction shocker *Invisible Invaders* and Alfred Hitchcock's exemplary *The Birds* (1963), *Night of the Living Dead* was written by Romero and John Russo, partners in Latent Image, an advertising company producing television commercials and ephemeral films for various Pittsburgh-based industries. Together with a third partner, Russell Streiner, they contacted one such local company, Hardman Associates, with the intention of setting up a production unit to develop, finance and produce a low-budget horror movie. Image Ten was duly formed by Romero, Russo and Streiner, along with Karl Hardman and Marilyn Eastman from Hardman Associates, and a tight budget of $114,000 was secured.

Much of the filming took place at weekends to accommodate the group's regular Monday-to-Friday jobs and, as with *The Evil Dead*, with few resources available to them Romero and his team adopted a hands-on approach which would prove not only economical but creatively constructive. Shot in harsh black-and-white, featuring a mostly non-professional cast in principal roles – only Duane Jones and Judith O'Dea had any concrete acting experience – *Night of the Living Dead* wickedly takes the accepted conventions of the horror genre and shakes them up before scattering them in a wonderful pattern.

Fig. 3 George A. Romero's Night of the Living Dead.

The dead return to life and attack the living for no discernible reason. The apparent hero, Johnny (played by co-producer Russell Streiner) is attacked and killed by a zombie (or ghoul, as the script refers to them; zombies at the time were more commonly associated with Haitian voodoo practices, but the word took on a very different connotation following the success of Romero's film). The heroine, Barbra (Judith O'Dea) is reduced to an exhausted wreck after narrowly escaping a similar fate. A nearby farmhouse might be able to provide sanctuary for her as she flees the ghoul (Bill Hinzman) but the sole occupant appears to be a decayed corpse. As night falls a man, Ben (Duane Jones, a black actor cast simply because he was best that Romero could find to fill the role, but who inadvertently created the genre's first black hero) arrives at the farmhouse and proceeds to secure the property against the hordes of zombies that have begun to gather outside (the shuffling ghouls are mostly played by crew friends and fellow financiers). Alerted by the noise upstairs, a gang of survivors emerge from the cellar and plan their escape, but this only results in disagreement, anger and needless death. The radio and television news reports confusion, and social institutions are as dumbfounded as everyone else (allusions are made to radiation fallout as the probable cause of the impending zombie apocalypse but Romero wisely sidesteps the issue). Finally, the film becomes arguably the first American film in any genre to comment – albeit obliquely – upon the escalating crisis of the war in South-East Asia and the disgraceful involvement of the US military in the massacre of Vietnamese civilians at Thuy

Bo and My Lai: at dawn an armed posse led by the local sheriff (George Kosana, another of the film's investors) shoot Ben – who had concealed himself in the cellar when the farmhouse became overrun with ghouls and the other members of the group had been killed or devoured – whom they confuse for one of the many zombies they are now dispatching with a bullet to the head ('They're dead... they're all messed up').

The chiaroscuro photography – as well as directing and co-writing Romero also served as cinematographer and editor – and rough-and-ready hand-held approach inform the film with an almost documentary-like hyper-realism, enhanced further by the effective use of news broadcasts and on-location interviews – 'Everything is being done that can be done', says one government official, while the sheriff displays a remarkable nonchalance when discussing how to deal with the zombies that are now lumbering around the countryside ('Shoot 'em in the head, that's a sure way to kill 'em... or beat 'em or burn 'em, they go up pretty easy').

Night of the Living Dead was acquired for distribution by the Walter Reade Organization, a New York-based company who distributed a range of domestic and foreign films in the US, among them *Monsieur Hulot's Holiday* (*Les vacances de Monsieur Hulot*, 1952) and others by the French actor-director Jacques Tati, John Cassavetes' *Faces* (1968) and Gordon Flemyng's *Daleks: Invasion Earth 2150 A.D.* (1966). Whilst other potential distributors, including Samuel Z. Arkoff and James H. Nicholson's American International Pictures (AIP), balked at the level of gore and the bleak *dénouement*, company president Walter Reade Jr. agreed to release the film uncut, insisting only upon a title change (*Night of the Flesh Eaters* instead became *Night of the Living Dead* to avoid any confusion with Jack Curtis' sci-fi horror *The Flesh Eaters*, 1963).

Following its premiere in October 1968 a review of the film which was published in the American entertainment magazine *Variety* draws neat parallels with the British media's later attitude towards *The Evil Dead* and the 'video nasty' phenomenon:

> Until the Supreme Court establishes clear-cut guidelines for the pornography of violence, *Night of the Living Dead* will serve nicely as an outer-limit example... this horror film casts serious aspersions on the integrity and social responsibility of its Pittsburgh-based makers, distributor Walter Reade, the film industry as a whole and [exhibitors] who book [the picture], as well as raising doubts about the future of the

regional cinema movement and the moral health of filmgoers who cheerfully opt for this unrelieved orgy of sadism. (quoted in Russell 2008: 65)

In the UK, *Night of the Living Dead* was passed with cuts for an 'X' rating by the British Board of Film Censors (BBFC) in June 1969, for release by Monarch Films.

There are some stimulating parallels between the production of *Night of the Living Dead* and that of *The Evil Dead*. The farmhouse located outside Evans City, Pennsylvania, which would serve as the primary site of the undead activity in Romero's film, was a condemned building and marked down for demolition. The cabin in the woods in *The Evil Dead* was also in a poor, uninhabitable state, but at least Raimi's team could retreat to more comfortable hotel lodgings at the end of each working day or night. This was not the case for Romero and his equally inexperienced and cash-strapped crew: they slept in the farmhouse, mostly in cots but sometimes on the floor, and as there was no water supply they had to wash in a nearby creek. There was also a genuine fear that their equipment could be stolen from the farmhouse if it was left unprotected, and so living on the premises became a vital necessity. While filming *The Evil Dead* in Tennessee, unknown perpetrators helped themselves to some expensive equipment which Raimi's team had stored at the cabin; to prevent further thefts the crew acted as security guards for the remainder of the shoot.

Due to the tightness of the respective budgets and the sometimes haphazard way in which both films were shot in awkward, fraught conditions, *Night of the Living Dead* and *The Evil Dead* are superb examples of communal filmmaking. The phrase 'do-it-yourself' has never been better applied than here; in both instances the casts are as active behind the camera as in front of it, various production duties (manual operations, catering, driving, even minor stunt-work) are shared across the board and Romero and Raimi help to create an environment in which everyone is made to feel that they have a part to play, with no tedious committee meetings to attend and no disruptive egos to generate discord.

'Romero took the genre out of its gothic castles and swept away its cobwebs,' notes Jon Towlson. '*Night of the Living Dead* marked a transition in horror cinema, from the classic to the modern' (Towlson 2018, online). What made *Night of the Living Dead* resonate so strongly in the late 1960s and early 1970s was the successful attempt by Romero to crack the earth open and plant a new and powerful seed. It introduced the zombie as the eternal allegorical monster, replaced the standard good-overcomes-evil ending with one of despair and hopelessness (perfectly capturing the social and political turbulence of the period), and proved conclusively that over-inflated budgets are no match for imagination and ingenuity. Although *Night of the Living Dead* transformed the genre in a way that has never been achieved since, *The Evil Dead* was influential in its own right (this will be examined in Chapter 6). But where the Raimi and Romero films converge is in their never-say-die attitude in the face of adversity, and a total commitment to creating a work that is singular, visceral, convention challenging, and never to be forgotten.

RESURRECTING THE SPIRIT OF H.P. LOVECRAFT

In addition to the early works of George Romero, Tobe Hooper and Wes Craven, Rob Tapert also suggested that the script of *Within the Woods* make some reference to Sumerian religion, the most ancient of all religious practices which originated around 4000 B.C. in the region of Mesopotamia (now Iraq). This struck a chord with Raimi:

> My ancient history professor was giving a dissertation on Sumerian culture... and she mentioned the ancient Sumerian Book of the Dead, which is actually a series of scrolls and not one bound book. They were about burial rites, funerary incantations and passages explaining the trip to the netherworlds beyond death, and that suddenly pricked up my ears. (Raimi in Warren 2000: 36)

Another notable point of reference was the work of H.P. Lovecraft, in particular 'The Necronomicon' ('Kitab al-Azif'), an alchemical text which first appears in Lovecraft's 1921 short story 'The Nameless City'. The Great Old Ones (monstrous, God-like creatures from another world, once powerful on Earth but now hidden and awaiting the call to rise once again) are the supernatural forces behind a number of Lovecraft's weird tales, a strand of fiction known as the 'Cthulhu Mythos' ('The Call of Cthulhu', 1926, 'The Dunwich Horror', 1928, 'At the Mountains of Madness', 1931, and 'The Case of Charles Dexter Ward', 1941, among others). Following Lovecraft's death in 1937, the world of the Mythos would expand and provide inspiration to other authors thanks to the example set by August Derleth, Lovecraft's frequent collaborator, whose own contributions can be found in the collections *The Mask of Cthulhu* (1958) and *The Trail of Cthulhu* (1962). Other post-Lovecraft/Derleth explorations include novels by Brian Lumley (*The Borrowers Beneath*, 1974), Graham Masterton (*The Manitou*, 1976), F. Paul Wilson (*The Keep*, 1981) and stories by Ramsey Campbell ('The Inhabitant of the Lake', 1964) and Stephen King ('Jerusalem's Lot', 1978, a short prequel of sorts in epistolary form to his 1975 novel *'Salem's Lot*).

SUPER-8 NIGHTMARES: *CLOCKWORK* AND *WITHIN THE WOODS*

Fig. 4 Sam Raimi's Clockwork.

Clockwork, shot around New Year 1979, was Sam Raimi's first tentative stab at directing a horror movie. A seven-minute intruder-in-the-house story featuring Cheryl Guttridge (later a 'Fake Shemp', or double, in *The Evil Dead*) being awoken in the night by a knife-wielding madman (Scott Spiegel), it's technically proficient even if it amounts to very little.

Spiegel and Bruce Campbell had flirted with horror some years earlier. Remembers Spiegel:

> Actually in 1974 Bruce and I did a five minute werewolf film called *Curse of the Werewolf* (we loved stealing titles!). Bruce and I wrote it and acted in it and I directed it. I played the werewolf. There was a cool shot in the film where the camera is over my hairy werewolf arm and my hand is outstretched and we follow it through the

woods in a long tracking shot as we see Bruce in the distance and then we come upon Bruce, who plays a hunter, and he turns in shock as I grab his throat and strangle him relentlessly with my hand and throw him to the ground where he coughs up lots of blood. The same year Bruce directed himself, me and Matt Taylor in a serious suspense thriller entitled *Manhunt*. It had violence and thrills... it's a nifty little movie and was a total departure from the comedies we were doing at the time. Then in 1976 we did the 16mm short *Mystery No Mystery*. It had creepy and scary moments with surreal, Ernie Kovacs-style comedy. Sam and I wrote it, Sam directed it, and Bruce and I starred in it. Then later, we did a Super-8 version. This led to *It's Murder* a couple of years later. And that led to *Clockwork*. Sam wrote the script, Rob Tapert produced and Cheryl Guttridge and I starred. We shot it over a weekend at Sam's house. Bruce had to double my arms bursting through the door, because we were using a real knife, and I said 'I can't do this, it's a real knife and I might hurt her!' So Bruce became my 'stunt' arms. I did a very painful stunt falling down the stairs (with a bloody knife prop in my mouth no less). Every time I see that fall it still hurts my tail bone. (Spiegel 2011, online)

A short gestation period followed, during which time Raimi and Rob Tapert speculated about using *Within the Woods* as a kind of advertisement, or 30-minute trailer, which they hoped would stimulate enough of an interest to supply the financing for a feature-length film. With his academic pedigree proving to be an invaluable asset, Tapert began searching for probable future investment in a horror movie (at this point the working title was *Book of the Dead*).

Fig 5. Ellen discovers what has become of Bruce in Within the Woods.

In the cool spring of 1979, with the script complete and now intending to use the film to encourage the financial stimulus for *Book of the Dead*, Raimi shot *Within the Woods* on a budget of $1,600 using only Super-8 stock and equipment over a period of six days at the Michigan farmhouse owned by the Tapert family.

Within the Woods opens with Raimi's camera prowling through an eerie woodland before racing into a barn and around the grounds of a whitewashed farmhouse, where the front porch swings repeatedly and ominously against the outer wall. The occupants are bespectacled Bruce (Bruce Campbell), Ellen (Ellen Sandweiss), Scotty (Scott Spiegel) and Mary (Mary Valenti). Bruce and Ellen head out for an afternoon picnic. Bruce explains to Ellen that the place they are visiting is 'part of an old Indian burial ground, very sacred and holy'. Ellen asks if the area is cursed, but Bruce allays her fears by telling her that 'you're only cursed by the evil spirits if you violate the graves of the dead'. While Ellen prepares the food Bruce looks for firewood, but his digging unearths a strange wooden cross and a dagger which he believes is a 200-year-old Indian relic. Ellen feels uneasy about their close proximity to the ancient dead, although Bruce dismisses both the legend and the knife; the couple appear oblivious to the fire which bursts into life from the ground where Bruce has been digging.

Waking from a nap Ellen notices that Bruce has gone. She calls out to him while searching the forest. Something causes her to trip and fall and when she looks up she is confronted with the mutilated corpse of her boyfriend hanging upside down from a tree. An unseen presence, with a horrifying guttural roar, pursues the frantic, screaming Ellen through woods and streams before she makes it back to the farmhouse. The 'thing' finally retreats as she reaches sanctuary. The hand which suddenly seizes her in the doorway is revealed to be Scotty, who decides to search the forest as night begins to descend, leaving a distraught Ellen alone with Mary.

When Scotty fails to return Mary ventures to the edge of the forest hoping to meet him on his way back, but she is attacked by the now demonic Bruce, who grabs her by the throat and raises her up off the ground. 'Join us,' he growls, before stabbing her through the neck. Ellen raids the kitchen searching for a weapon. Armed with a pair of knives, she is disturbed by the rattle of the front door knob. As the door opens she stabs whom she believes to be Bruce, only for Scotty to stagger in, mortally wounded.

Demon Bruce is already inside the house; as he makes a grab for Ellen she slams the door shut on his hand and succeeds in warding him off with several stabs to the withered limb. Bruce manages to break free and admonishes Ellen with a menacing threat – 'You have violated the ancient ways and so must die... To join...' Ellen stabs again at his hand as he seizes her neck but Bruce tears off what remains of it. A struggle follows during which Bruce is finally dispatched with the same ancient dagger he had discovered in the woods earlier that day. The film ends with a clear visual reference to *Halloween* with the now-possessed Scotty sitting bolt upright behind the foregrounded Ellen as she weeps hysterically.

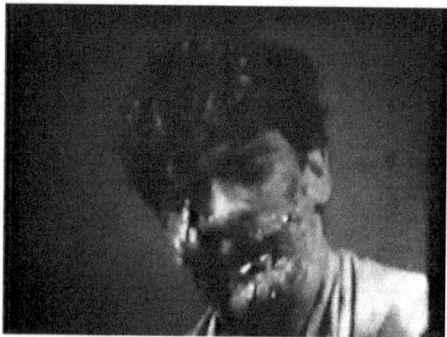

Fig 6. Demon Bruce in Within the Woods.

Taken as both a short horror film in its own right and a companion piece to *The Evil Dead*, just how effective is *Within the Woods*? It is certainly gruesome and doesn't flinch from showing as much gore as the budget and running time will allow. The special make-up effects were created by Tom Sullivan, a talented artist who had previously collaborated with Sam Raimi on *It's Murder* (1978). On this film and *The Evil Dead* he displays a fondness for scary faces – the pasty, blood-streaked visages of the possessed Bruce and Scotty in *Within the Woods* and, in particular, Cheryl in *The Evil Dead*, are genuinely nightmarish; he would excel himself with his elaborate work on *The Evil Dead* despite working with limited time and money. The photography by Tim Philo – who would also graduate to *The Evil Dead* – and the public domain musical score are also worthy of note. Raimi makes creepy use of the springtime locations, with the camera gliding through the trees and the farmhouse outbuildings as the point-of-view of an unseen threatening force. In conjunction with the vivid imagery, the stock music helps to generate an unsettling effect; in spite of its familiarity it does seem appropriate - as is also the case with *Night of the Living Dead*, which lifts its soundtrack from, among others, Robert Clarke's *The Hideous Sun Demon* (1958) and Tom Graeff's *Teenagers from Outer Space* (1958). According to Scott Spiegel, *Within the Woods* uses 'cuts from *Death Wish*, the 1978 version of *Invasion of the Body Snatchers*, *Sorcerer*, *Jaws* and *The Eyes of Laura Mars*' (Spiegel 2011, online), and it often suits the mood and atmosphere quite smartly.

Scott Spiegel has good memories of the shoot:

> It was great. Just a small cast and crew. We shot it over several weekends at Rob Tapert's parents' place in Marshall, Michigan. I remember I'd grab several props from the grocery store, some knives, the cherry pie filling that Mary Valenti spits out when Bruce stabs her in the throat. I remember when Ellen stabs me we had a 'half' knife that they duct taped to my torso. When we finished the scene I had to rip the tape off my hairy chest and I screamed bloody murder. It was cool to be made up by Tom Sullivan. He is so talented. I loved the way I looked as a monster in that film (and I get to have a great 'pop up' scare at the end). The guys made a horror classic and I was proud to be a part of it. (Spiegel 2011, online)

Within the Woods is not without its faults. The weather just seems too damn chilly for Bruce and Ellen to be taking a picnic and the acting too often verges on the melodramatic (Bruce's death throes are particularly overcooked). One way of looking at *Within the Woods* is as the Super-8 equivalent of a 'demo' track, cut by a musical artist to pitch to a record publisher or label or to try out an arrangement or structure for the first time before entering the studio to record the song for a single or album. *Within the Woods* can be considered one such demo recording, a prototype, a 30-minute teaser trailer, if you will, for *The Evil Dead*. With this in mind, its faults can be forgiven.

How does it compare in relation to its big brother? Firstly, the main similarities. Bruce, Ellen, Scotty and Mary are essentially the same characters which appear in *The Evil Dead*, albeit with Bruce and Mary becoming known as Ash and Shelly respectively and Ellen's name being changed to Linda, but with the addition in *The Evil Dead* of a fifth member, Cheryl. Characterisation in both films is kept to a threadbare minimum, as though Raimi is unsure how to populate his story with relevant or even believable protagonists. Both

Within the Woods and *The Evil Dead* open with POV shots as the Force prowls across a small lake, through bushes and trees, and emerging out of the forest. In *The Evil Dead* the camerawork during these scenes is more fluid, faster and aggressive, suggesting that the Force (or whatever it may be that lurks within the woods) is far more powerful.

Bruce discovers an ancient dagger, as Ash will do in the later film, and this is put to devastating use during the climactic battle between Ellen and the possessed Bruce. Ancient spirits are unwittingly called forth, not through the playback of unholy incantations, but in more mundane fashion in *Within the Woods*, that of removing sacred objects from a burial site. The same actress (Ellen Sandweiss) is pursued through the forest in each film but *Within the Woods* does not feature an equivalent 'tree rape', only a big jolt as Scotty clutches her wrist after she drops her keys to the farmhouse door (it's Ash who grabs her in the later film). When Bruce reappears, now possessed and intent on murdering his former friends, he invites the others to 'join us', as does the demonic Cheryl in *The Evil Dead*.

Bruce/Ash takes front and centre stage in both movies, and it's this character who provides the crucial difference between *Within the Woods* and *The Evil Dead*. In *The Evil Dead* Ash is the reluctant hero, called into violent action despite having neither the stomach nor the courage for bodily dismemberment. But in *Within the Woods* there is a reversal of roles: Bruce is now the one who becomes possessed, leaving Ellen to fight back and to show the determination and bravery needed to vanquish the demon before it can compel her, through her own brutal death, to become one of 'them'. We never do learn Mary's fate in *Within the Woods*, but it is fairly safe to assume that, like Scotty, she too will be reanimated after death.

Sam Raimi considers the film the 'halfway point between our Super-8 movies and a professional, low-budget, feature-length movie' (Raimi in Warren 2000: 38), and even makes the case for it being a more satisfying horror film than *The Evil Dead*: 'It was more effective at making the audience scream than *Evil Dead* was, so in that way it was better. But it wasn't as professionally photographed, the sound wasn't as good, and the image quality wasn't as good, since it was Super-8, I think it did manipulate the audience better, providing more of an experience like John Carpenter did with *Halloween*' (Raimi in Warren 2000: 40). Reviewing the film in the *Detroit News* (24th August 1979), Michael

McWilliams was suitably impressed with Raimi's small-scale shocker:

> It will probably never be advertised alongside the glossy, big-budget horror movies of our time, but you won't easily forget a locally produced little film called *Within the Woods*. In just thirty-two minutes, it provides more chills, thrills and squeamish giggles than such recent professional duds as *Prophecy* and *The Amityville Horror* combined. [Raimi] has looked at *Night of the Living Dead* and knows our terror of the grave. He has looked at *Carrie* and knows the effect of a bloody arm out of the blue. He has looked at *Taxi Driver* and knows the sometimes-psychotic rites of 'manhood'. He has looked at *The Texas Chainsaw Massacre* and knows our primal fascination with blood. Raimi displays a wealth of learning in *Within the Woods*. Perhaps he will be able to make a more extended work, a feature film, in which he can clear up some of his technical deficiencies and prove that he has the personal depth to provide a context – a thematic meaning – for all his gore. (McWilliams in Warren 2000: 43-44)

And with this endorsement Sam Raimi, Bruce Campbell and Rob Tapert began to mould and develop what they considered their pet project, one which they hoped would lead to greater things. But first there were many obstacles for the trio to overcome before the cameras could start rolling.

NOTES

1. Raimi's 17 Super-8 short films are as follows:
   Out West (1972)
   The Great Bogus Monkey Pignuts Swindle (1975, starring Campbell)
   The James R. Hoffa Story Part II (1976, co-directed by Spiegel, starring Campbell)
   Attack of the Pillsbury Doughboy (1976, co-directed by Spiegel)
   Uncivil War Birds (1976, starring Campbell)
   Mystery No Mystery (1976, co-directed by Spiegel, starring Campbell)
   Picnic (1977, co-directed by Spiegel, starring Campbell)
   Charlie's Angels (1977, co-directed by Spiegel, a spoof of the ABC television series)
   The Kids' Film (1977, co-directed by Spiegel)
   Six Months to Live (1977, co-directed by Spiegel, starring Campbell)
   The Happy Valley Kid (1977, starring Campbell and Spiegel)
   Lonely Are the Brave (1977)

Civil War Part II (1977, starring Campbell and Spiegel)
It's Murder (1978, starring Campbell and Spiegel)
William Shakespeare: The Movie (1979, starring Campbell)
Clockwork (1979, starring Spiegel)
Within the Woods (1979, starring Campbell and Spiegel)

A late runner, *The Happy Sap*, starring Spiegel and Campbell, appeared in 1985, the same year as Raimi's second feature, *Crimewave*. In addition, Raimi would have acting roles in the following 15 Super-8's, collaborating further with Campbell, Spiegel and Becker:
No Dough Boys (1974, directed by Spiegel)
I'll Never Heil Again (1975, directed by Spiegel and Campbell)
The James R. Hoffa Story (1975, directed by Spiegel and Campbell)
James Bombed in Here Today... Gun Tomorrow (1976, directed by Spiegel, a 007 parody as the title suggests)
Topanga Pearl (1976, directed by Becker)
Final Round (1977, directed by Becker)
Holding It (1978, directed by Becker)
Shemp Eats the Moon (1978, directed by John Cameron)
Attack of the Helping Hand (1979, directed by Spiegel)
Night Crew (1979, directed by Spiegel)
Spring Cleaning (1979, directed by Campbell)
Fish Sticks (1979, directed by Campbell)
The Blind Waiter (1979, directed by Spiegel and Becker)
Stryker's War (1980, directed by Becker)
Cleveland Smith, Bounty Hunter (1982, directed by Becker and Spiegel)

2. Josh Becker, employed on the film as a PA (production assistant) kept an informative journal of his experiences on *Book of the Dead*, a copy of which can be found on the equally informative and exhaustive Book Of The Dead website – www.bookofthedead.ws – and in longer form in Becker's 2008 book *Rushes*.

Chapter 2: The Ultimate Experience in Gruelling Terror

Raising Money to Raise the Dead

The first public screening of *Within the Woods* took place at Detroit's Punch & Judy cinema in August 1979, propping up Jim Sharman's *The Rocky Horror Picture Show* (1975), which had become a tremendous success running the midnight movie circuit in the United States. The audience reaction to Sam Raimi's mini film was favourable despite technical problems: due to the low power output of the Super-8 projector the equipment had to be moved to the centre of the main aisle and even then the image filled roughly only a quarter of the screen.

Now the complicated legal and financial proceedings would need to be confronted if Raimi, Rob Tapert and Bruce Campbell were to progress with *The Evil Dead*. The Tapert family lawyer, Phil Gillis, was instrumental in assisting the trio's familiarisation with the fiscal factors of investment, sponsorship and budgetary concerns, even if the finer detail went completely above their heads. Says Campbell:

> He [Gillis] wound up being pretty much the guardian angel of the whole project. He said he wanted $20,000 for his work, but he essentially folded it back into the film, and another $80,000 as well; he wound up putting about $100,000 into it. And the young guy who did the legal work on the limited partnership was Brian Manoogian; his family is related to the Masco Corporation, a Fortune 500 company, which makes Delta faucets. And he invested too, as did his brother, a friend of his and his sister. Between Phil Gillis and Manoogian, we got about two-thirds of our money. (Campbell in Warren 2000: 45)

It was Phil Gillis and Brian Manoogian who formally created the *The Evil Dead*'s production company (the 'limited partnership' that Bruce Campbell speaks of), Renaissance Pictures, in August of 1979, soon after the public premiere of *Within the Woods*. The original intention was to shoot *The Evil Dead* in Super-8, a format which the Renaissance trio felt more than comfortable with, and then blow it up to 35mm.

Raimi decided on a test run: a Super-8 short, *Terror at Lulu's* (filmed at his mother's lingerie shop) was quickly put together, blown up to 35mm, and viewed by the team at a local cinema, the Maple. At the very least, they hoped, the film would look like a 16mm enlargement, but the results were unsatisfactory, if not calamitous. The blow-up had created grain 'the size of hailstones', remembers Rob Tapert, 'it was unwatchable, unreleasable' (Tapert in Warren 2000: 46). He suggested that it would be more feasible to shoot *The Evil Dead* in 16mm, a wise decision which they would benefit from enormously in the months to come, especially as their experience with *Terror at Lulu's* had left them deflated and unsure of whether to continue with the project or abandon it altogether.

But still the difficult subject of investment had to be addressed. The Renaissance group already had a prototype model in place to prove to investors that they were competent filmmakers, and a brief synopsis had been typed up ready to be handed out at meetings with interested parties.

'*Something evil is lurking about the wooded mountains of Tennessee,*' begins Raimi's synopsis, and in just a few short paragraphs he describes a story outline that mirrors fairly closely the finished film. '*As the evil force grows stronger, one by one the vacationers become possessed by it. Their eyes turn bone white and their bodies are jerked about like marionettes as they are driven to kill their own friends and lovers. Struggle after struggle, battle after battle, the dwindling number of humans continue to destroy the white eyed possessed until only one man remains.*' Perhaps sensing that a positive resolution would be attractive to investors, the sole survivor '*walks off into the mists of the early morning hours to safety*' (how less effective, and dramatic, this conclusion would have been had the team opted to film it as originally conceived) (Raimi quoted in Warren 2000: 205).

Following further discussions amongst lawyers Phil Gillis, Brian Manoogian and accountant Charlie Bosler, a budget was agreed of $150,000. After doing the rounds, engaging with potential investors (some known already to the group, others complete strangers), screening *Within the Woods* for them and explaining their intentions for *The Evil Dead*, they had raised $85,000 (57%), still $65,000 short of the required target. The Renaissance partners were eager to begin filming as soon as possible, but there was a major obstacle blocking the woodland trail: the funds had been deposited into an escrow account, the conditions of which meant that the money could not be accessed until nine of the Renaissance shares had been sold. Fortunately, the investors agreed to release the funds, although by this time the proposed shooting schedule which was to have commenced in the summer of 1979 had long gone and winter was drawing near. This would, however, turn out to be perfect for the film – it's hard to imagine *The Evil Dead* generating quite the same atmosphere in glorious summertime, although it would certainly prove to be uncomfortable, sometimes even painful, for the cast and crew.

Fake Names, Fake Shemps

As the story revolves around just five characters, casting decisions were fairly straightforward. Bruce Campbell would play the film's male lead, Ash, essentially reprising his role from *Within the Woods*, albeit with a few significant variations. As his sister Cheryl, Ellen Sandweiss had appeared in John Cameron's Super-8 short *Shemp Eats the Moon* (1978, also starring Campbell and Sam Raimi) and, crucially, *Within the Woods*. Sandweiss would go on to appear with Campbell again in the self-reflexive *My Name Is Bruce* (2006) and two episodes of the television series *Ash vs. Evil Dead* (2015 – 2018). Betsy Baker was cast as Ash's girlfriend Linda, Richard DeManincor successfully auditioned as Scott and Theresa Seyferth (Charlie Bosler's daughter) landed the part of Scott's girlfriend Shelly; all three were Michigan natives. However, DeManincor and Seyferth were members of the Screen Actors Guild and, under the guidelines set out by the SAG, they were entitled to a basic minimum wage. Renaissance simply could not afford to pay scale so a little dishonesty was called for: Seyferth became 'Sarah York', while DeManincor hid behind the pseudonym 'Hal Delrich' (DeManincor appears briefly, under his own name, in Raimi's *Crimewave*).

Recalls Theresa Seyferth on being credited as 'Sarah York':

> I used a fake name in *The Evil Dead*; I went from Theresa Seyferth to Sarah York, as I was unable to work out a compromise with the producers and SAG. I was fearful of the consequences, although none of us ever believed this movie would see the light of day. As luck would have it, a few people saw the movie and I was suspended from SAG and fired... My very first SAG job was literally two months prior to shooting *The Evil Dead*. If that situation were to happen today both SAG and the producers would most certainly try to work out a Low Budget contract. I was young and had

no skill-set for dealing with authoritarian bureaucracies; I was intimidated by both and therefore found a solution by creating a different identity. (Seyferth 2019, online)

Up to 20 people would be identified, at various stages of the production, as 'Fake Shemps', including Raimi and Tapert (who can be glimpsed as fishermen by the roadside in the early scenes), Phil Gillis, Scott Spiegel and Sam's brothers, Ted and Ivan. The concept of the 'Fake Shemp' (a body double or stand-in) is derived from the Three Stooges: following the untimely death of Shemp Howard in 1955, the remaining Stooges, Moe Howard and Larry Fine, used another actor (Joe Palma, a Stooges regular), to double for him in order to complete four short films which were in production at the same time (*Commotion on the Ocean*, *Hot Stuff*, *Rumpus in the Harem* and *Scheming Schemers*, all directed by Jules White and released in 1956). Explains Bill Warren, 'Stooge fans Sam, Scott and Bruce spotted these fake Shemps immediately, and when they found it necessary to have someone double for another actor (often for many others)... they called the doubles "Fake Shemps"' (Warren 2000: 31). For example, in *The Evil Dead*, when demon Linda rises from the grave she is played by Cheryl Guttridge but other shots in this sequence feature Barbara Carey, a local Tennessean, doubling for the unavailable Betsy Baker.

'Fake Shemping' was an adventure for Cheryl Guttridge, but not always a pleasurable one:

> When the boys got back from the shoot in Tennessee, they realised they still needed some pickup shots. I don't know if the original actresses were unavailable or if I was the only one willing to work for a Big Mac and fries, but Rob called and asked if I could help them. I spent a good part of the summer before starting college at Sam's parents' house doing all sorts of odd 'acting' jobs, like the scene where I had to come up out of the ground spitting blood out of my mouth. It was shot in Sam's garage and it was about 120 degrees. I was covered in waxy, thick pancake make-up, was wearing a really hot and scratchy wig and had white contacts in my eyes. I took a slug of this gross mix of ketchup and karo syrup, crawled into a coffin-like box and held my breath while they piled 'dirt' on top of me. I remember lying there and hearing Bruce yell out – 'I think now's a good time to tell you that the dirt is really horse manure!' I asked Rob years later if that was true and he said it wasn't real dirt because

it would've been too heavy for me to push through, but he was 'pretty sure' they used peat moss – not manure. Whatever it was, it got into my eyes, my mouth, my nose – ugh. By far the worst scene for me though, was the one where that disease type infection goes up the girl's leg. That was done with stop-motion photography and I had to lie in one position (without moving) while the make-up artist drew a tiny bit on my leg, then stopped so they could take a picture... drew a tiny bit more, then stopped... it took hours and hours. It was incredibly difficult to stay completely still. (Guttridge 2009, online)

Sam Raimi's 14-year-old brother Ted enjoyed himself helping out on location but seemed oblivious to the latent dangers of being a 'Fake Shemp':

There was a couple of things that I did that I don't think anybody but a young teenager like myself would have done. I crawled underneath the cabin, with dirt, plywood, rusty nails, all kinds of crap, to have my hands flying out to the floorboards at Bruce's face. We found that as the floorboards were so hard, they had to be scored to allow me to punch through. Dart [construction supervisor Steve Frankel] used a skill saw to cut a star shape into the wood, so when my hands come bursting through it would splinter. Unfortunately I was so stuck underneath that cabin, that there wasn't time to have me crawl back out, so as Dart made the cuts, I could see the blade moving, maybe three or four inches from my eyes! (Ted Raimi 2013, online)

Logistically, Michigan would make the ideal location for all exterior and interior shooting, as well as pre-production organisation and post-filming commitments; the main players were based in the state and local resources could be utilised where required. However, Michigan winters are notoriously cold so the Renaissance partners had to make a decision: tolerate the freezing cold or choose a location further south where hopefully the weather would be milder. Tennessee was selected as the principal filming location (it had already been mentioned in Raimi's handout); the deep forest environment would help to create the right mood and tempo that they were looking for. Unfortunately, the mild winter the team were expecting did not materialise – Tennessee was to endure its coldest winter for several decades.

One of the many headaches the group had to tolerate was the question of payment. Only two of the cast were professional, in the sense that they were both members of the SAG, but everyone else involved (and that included Raimi, Tapert and Campbell) were essentially amateurs, virgins when it came to feature film making and perhaps a trifle unsure of both themselves and their pet project. Whenever a movie budget is drawn up it needs to be broken down and a certain percentage allocated to each vital element of the production. It was decided that the actors would be paid $100 per week. The Renaissance partners agreed to pay themselves $35 each but according to Bruce Campbell it went straight back into the film. Originally the shooting schedule was set at six weeks but this was eventually extended to 12 as several crew members had to depart at various times due to prior commitments. And so, on Sunday 11th November 1979, armed with a 66-page script (at that length more a rough draft than a complete shooting script) the Renaissance team set off on the 10-hour, 600-mile journey from Michigan to Tennessee.

THE CABIN IN THE WOODS

Fig. 7 The group arrive at their final destination.

Two days after arriving in Tennessee, the movie's centrepiece had been procured: an abandoned log cabin in the woods outside Morristown, located in Hamblen County approximately 226 miles from the state capital, Nashville. The Tennessee Film Commission had secured a cabin prior to their arrival but this proved to be unavailable when the owners declined the use of their property, so with the help of Gary Holt, a local character and Vietnam veteran, a new location was found which had the look, feel and smell of a house long since given over to the elements. Remembers Bruce Campbell:

> It had a power box but no power, no running water, it was just an abandoned cabin in a beautiful hollow. But it was a really cool area, very convenient. We blazed a new road because it was all overgrown, ran power in there, took out all the ceilings in the main room and tore out the middle wall. We had to tear out the ceilings because we needed to light from above, and hung the lights. After we scraped all the cow manure off, we found beautiful tongue-and-groove flooring. We had to build a trapdoor, and had to dig a cellar of sorts. We knew we could use the Tapert farmhouse in Marshall, Michigan, to shoot the scenes set in the cellar, because it had a great dirt floor and rock walls all around. (Campbell in Warren 2000: 56-57)

In addition to the cabin – which dated back to 1860 and was reputed to be haunted by the ghost of the builder, who was struck by lightning while constructing the chimney (ironically the chimney is all that remains following the cabin's destruction by fire in 1982) – Gary Holt also found the cast and crew lodgings in Morristown where they could sleep, eat, rehearse and prepare for the daily shoot. Theresa Seyferth recalls the day-to-day location routine:

> The entire cast and crew lived together in a house about five miles from the location of the cabin. We all had duties beyond the acting or crew. And mostly all of us helped with cleaning, cooking and grocery shopping. There was a lot of late-night filming which made life complicated. We were all lacking sleep. I remember one night waking up in the living room and the footage from the dailies was just flipping around the reels and everyone dead asleep. (Seyferth 2019, online)

THE SHOOT

Shooting commenced on Wednesday 14th November. It was the sequence with Ash, Cheryl, Scott, Linda and Shelly driving across the rickety bridge that leads to the cabin. Actually, the Bluff Road Bridge was 30 miles away from the cabin, and like the cabin itself is long gone. According to Bruce Campbell the bridge was genuinely unsafe and ought to have been condemned.

Principal photography in Tennessee continued on-and-off until Sunday 27th January 1980. The first day of shooting in the cabin was 26th November and a crew member was required to remain on the premises at all times following the mysterious overnight theft of their power tools (the perpetrators clearly had no interest in the far more valuable cine equipment as they left behind a $20,000 Arriflex camera and $5,000 Nagra sound recorder). Sam Raimi storyboarded the whole film but didn't always feel the need to follow them with any degree of rigidity, improvising wherever it was felt necessary.

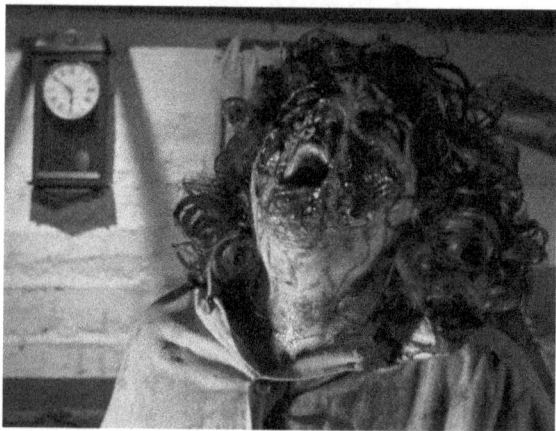

Fig. 8 Let the demonic possessions begin.

Conditions were harsh. The bitterly cold Tennessee winter, coupled with extremely long and unhealthy working hours, was hellish for everyone involved. Raimi encouraged his friends to dig in and contribute as much to the film creatively as they could conceivably manage, but tempers were frayed and morale was not always high. Ellen Sandweiss remembers the problems well:

> I scraped the hell out of myself. The make-up was also horrendous – because everything was so low-budget, everything really was an ordeal. We didn't quite have the right anything, whether it was the right make-up, or enough people to help with it. Those contacts in the eyes were really something. There was a lot of pain involved with that movie. There was pain with make-up, pain with running through woods… In the scene where I fall back into the cellar, at one point I didn't quite make it through the hole, and slammed my head on something. I remember how strange it was, staying up all night and sleeping through the day. I felt like a real zombie, but I was

20-years old, and it was very exciting, and I was with friends. (Sandweiss in Warren 2000: 66)

Theresa Seyferth recollects the filming of Shelly's gruesome dismemberment:

This may have been my worst night of shooting. Rob, Bruce and I were all nailed under the floor. Bruce and Rob played my arms and legs, maybe Teddy [Ted Raimi] too, they were my body parts strewn on the floor. I was the only one above the floor, but just my head. We were all nailed in and therefore unable to escape. Because my head was being filmed I needed to wear the lenses. We were sitting in dirt with spiders, worms, snakes and all things that live in the dirt! We shot for what seemed like a long time. At some point I wondered if Sam would ever say 'cut'. Finally in anguish and frustration from being entombed for so long, I dared to say something during the take, but there was no response from either Sam or Tim Philo the DP. It was then I realised they must have fallen asleep. Eventually my shouting woke them and they ended the scene and removed us from our tomb. (Seyferth 2019, online)

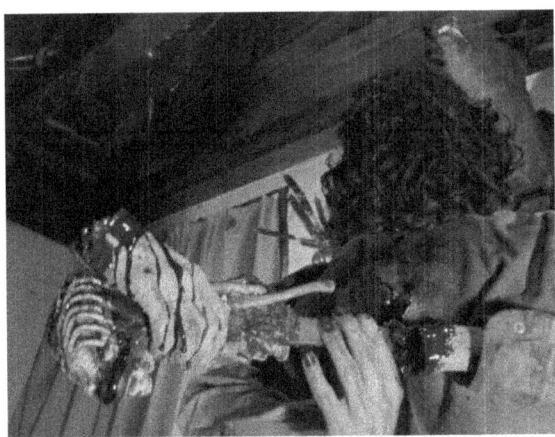

Fig. 9 The stabbing of Possessed Cheryl.

Relocating to Michigan, work could now begin on post-production, which involved all of the scenes (and a fair number of re-shoots) that they were unable to film on location in Tennessee. Among them were Cheryl's tree rape (shot at the Campbell family summer home); the scenes in the cellar and some of the cabin interior shots, which were lensed

Fig. 10 Cheryl dismembered.

at the Tapert farmhouse; the Force point-of-view sequence which opens the film; all of the extensive make-up effects sequences, along with a multitude of other shooting locations doubling for the cabin or the forest. The movie is so skilfully shot and edited that you simply cannot tell one site from another; for example, we're in the cabin in Tennessee when the cellar trapdoor flips open while the five friends are having dinner, but when Ash and Scott descend the steps to explore the dark cellar we're back in the Tapert family home in Michigan.

In order to continue filming (90% had been completed in Tennessee), additional funds needed to be secured from the investors, and this increased the final budget to between $350,000 to $400,000. In total, 100,000 feet of 16mm had been shot by Raimi and his Renaissance partners.

It's worth examining two elements of the movie which help to make *The Evil Dead* the horror classic that it is today. Raimi's creativity and enthusiasm had a profound effect on all his key collaborators, none more so than Tim Philo, the director of photography, and make-up effects artists Tom Sullivan and Bart Pierce.

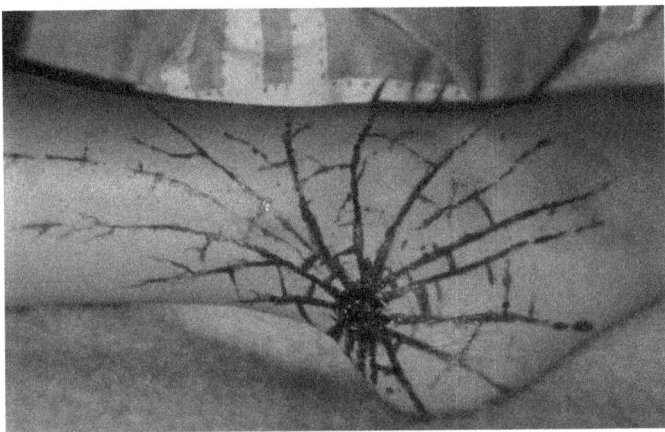

Fig. 11 A spider web of terror.

THE CINEMATOGRAPHY AND SPECIAL MAKE-UP EFFECTS OF *THE EVIL DEAD*

In *Within the Woods* Sam Raimi had utilised a number of POV shots from the perspective of the powerful yet invisible Force. Most effective are the scenes in which the Force careens at top-speed through the forest and the farmhouse outbuildings, its presence accompanied by guttural roaring on the soundtrack. *The Evil Dead* allowed Raimi the opportunity to develop, embellish and, crucially, have fun with the techniques that he had experimented with in the test model.

Michigan-based Tim Philo was brought on board as the film's cinematographer and, given that the team was forced to work with extremely limited resources, there is an enormous amount of inventiveness (not to mention playfulness) to Raimi and Philo's approach to *mise-en-scène*, camera angles, placement and composition. Bruce Campbell recalls this element of the production with fondness:

> Sam showed more savvy during the making of *Evil Dead* than I had ever seen before. I didn't know where he was getting all this nonsense, but it was finally his chance to use every trick he had learned to that point, and he just kept laying it on. Everything became a tricky shot, and his cameraman, Tim Philo, was up to it. We all kicked around

> a bunch of ideas on how to shoot some stuff, and that's how we got the idea for the 'Shaky-Cam'. That's a two-by-four with a guy on either end to stabilise it, the camera in the middle, you could go over bushes and logs, it was an incredibly versatile thing. (Campbell in Warren 2000: 58-59)

Tim Philo explains in more detail the 'Shaky-Cam' rig, and also the 'Vas-o-Cam', designed to create an improvised dolly effect:

> In talking with a filmmaker friend, we came to the idea of the 'Shaky-Cam'. He said that if you mount the camera on a long board and straddle the bannisters of a staircase, you could slide the camera down mimicking a crane shot. As we talked, we reasoned that the board itself, by its length, would lessen the amplitude of any wobble, at least along one axis of movement. Even a 24" board would create a smoother move than the 6" wide camera itself. Better yet (given coordinated operators) would be an 8" board. But in practice, the long board wouldn't work. For the wide-angle 'Force' effect we needed to pass close to trees and other things. The long board was abandoned and I think only one shot in the film used it. Sam had wanted the 'Force' shots of the evil entity to move through the woods knocking down trees as it went. We considered riding atop a bulldozer, keeping the blade of it out of frame, but seeing the effect of the trees falling from its power. This proved to be out of our reach, unsafe in plenty of ways. There was also the 'Vas-o-Cam' (the same board slid on top of another board with a greasy layer of petroleum jelly as lubricant), the 'Blank-o-Cam' (for a couple of low follow shots, I got carried, camera-forward, on a blanket pallbearer-style), plus we also had a wheelchair that we used for some running shots. These rigs sometimes helped to make the movie look like a movie. (Philo 2018, online)

The final results look superb, if a little rough around the edges when compared to the team's majestic work on the sequel, but shooting in such an inhospitable environment often meant that it wasn't easy attaining the desired effect. Philo outlines just one of the problems shooting on location:

> The worst of the experiences on location in Tennessee was working with the scleral contact lenses on the actors. The white lenses made the actors blind and were only supposed to be worn 15 minutes at a time, no more than five times a day. The

pressure was to shoot as many as four or five shots, sometimes in action sequences, with a blind actor (more often actress) who would be physically moved into position then coached into action verbally. This was in a shooting location without running water, and heated by a huge kerosene blower/heater. Hygiene was very difficult. (ibid.)

This brings us to the special make-up effects creations of Tom Sullivan and his assistant Bart Pierce. Sullivan had provided the gruesome effects for *Within the Woods* and so he knew exactly what Sam Raimi required, but his contribution to *The Evil Dead* went far beyond what was initially expected of him; he created the various props (the elaborately carved Kandarian dagger, the Book of the Dead, the necklace which Ash gifts to Linda), and Raimi admits that they 'simply could not have done the film without him' (Raimi in Warren 2000: 77).

Surprisingly, Tom Sullivan had no interest in horror until seeing George A. Romero's *Dawn of the Dead* (1978) for the first time. Remembers Sullivan:

> Growing up I avoided gory and violent films. I had read an article about *Night of the Living Dead* in *Reader's Digest* that declared it a weapon of mass destruction. I wouldn't even see James Bond films thinking I'd get warped. I got the job to do *The Evil Dead* and decided I should see what I was getting into. So I saw *Dawn of the Dead*. I was freaking out during the first 15 minutes until they land the chopper for more fuel and a zombie played by Jim Krut steps up on a box and his head is shaved off by the helicopter blades. I got it. This is actually fun. The rest of the film is a deft social satire so I was on the right track. And Tom Savini's effects are a banquet of great gags. (Sullivan 2010, online)

Tom Sullivan had already spent a few days at the cabin applying the special make-up and contact lenses for the actors. Explains Betsy Baker: 'The contact lenses were very uncomfortable, you were totally without sight when wearing them... and taking them out became a difficult task after 5–10 minutes, because your eyes were dry, inflamed, and your hands were dirty' (Baker 2019, online).

Richard DeManincor didn't have to endure the discomfort of the contact lenses and, unlike his female co-stars, he recalls the make-up process with fondness:

> As for input on my make-up, I just let Tom do what he wanted. He created all the looks. The 'facial cast' of me was really a full head cast. At the time Tom and Sam and Rob were pouring the gooey stuff all over my head and in my mouth, leaving straws in my nose to breathe... The result was a very good cast of my head which was used for the 'gouge my eyes out' scene. ...I never had to put the contact lenses in my eyes. By the time it came to do the shots where I had come back from the dead, the make-up that had been applied to my face so many times before it became something of a mask. Tom just glued the contacts into the eye holes in the mask. I felt bad for the girls who really did put opaque lenses in their eyes. Regardless, we were all blind while wearing those contacts. (DeManincor 2014, online)

Some effects sequences were filmed in Tennessee, for example the pencil stabbing, a hand chewing, and the scene in which Shelly's head catches fire and burns. Some scenes were rushed and didn't work anywhere near as effectively as they could have done given more time. Sullivan was disappointed with some of the results:

> When Deadite Cheryl is behind the front door, bursts through the door and grabs Ash, Ash turns and shoots Cheryl in the face. We see Cheryl take the force of the blast, tearing away part of her jaw. There is a large blood tube that can be seen. Sam had to crop the shot to remove more of the tube. The problem was that I had designed the effect to be easily and quickly reset for retakes. But being inexperienced and impatient with the special effects Rob Tapert and Sam didn't schedule the time to do it correctly and only allowed one take. (Sullivan 2010, online)

The bulk of the effects, however, needed to be worked on and completed during post-production in Michigan, and this included the elaborate demon meltdown. Bart Pierce recalls:

> My presentation was that I had two favourite meltdowns; *Horror of Dracula* [*Dracula*] with Christopher Lee dying at the end, and *The Time Machine* where you see the Morlock in stop motion disintegrate to a skeleton. Tom's favourite meltdown was the Morlock and he wanted to do the entire meltdown as stop motion, but my argument was what was really working in movies at that time, was things that were really gooey, ugly, like really gross... you had to [have] the ick or goo factor. Tom and I both animated... because at 48 frames for every second of film it was very time consuming.

Fig. 12 Scott's meltdown.

Of course we also shot Bruce in live-action. We couldn't afford to make any mistakes, everything had to be done correctly for each of the three to five passes for each shot, and if we got anything wrong we had to do it over again. My brother-in-law worked at a 7-Eleven convenience store. He had a video security camera which could tape one hour at a time. This was before VCRs, so in order to also be able to control split screens and match time, frame and film, I borrowed his security camera. We would aim this video camera at a scene, but we would be able to see the frame counter on screen and a clock in the larger frame background, and I would also count the seconds aloud, so they'd be recorded on the tape too. This would give us a recording which would show us exactly where actions happened. Then we re-wound the 16mm film to re-expose the next portion of the split screen, and we would play back the video camera footage for the next portion, so we had the exact timebase and verbal count as the previous one. We took Sam through the storyboards to show him what we had in mind, but we weren't sure up to that point if that would make him happy or not. Sam basically said, 'I have to pay off what I promised, throughout the entire movie, and you can't just make a film like this and not pay off with a gory end, all we want is the greatest meltdown that's ever been done'. (Pierce 2011, online)

Given just how intricate this sequence is, it's no wonder that Sullivan and Pierce storyboarded the whole piece, but they were given a free hand by Sam Raimi to compose the sequence entirely as they saw fit. The end result is unforgettably impressive.

Chapter 3: The 'Bad Dream' and the 'Bad Place' in *The Evil Dead*

> The subject of the 'uncanny'... is undoubtedly related to what is frightening – to what arouses dread and horror (Freud 1919/1985: 339)

The Bad Place

Horror in both literature and film is frequently associated with intense psychological states which arouse 'eerie, weird... gruesome fear' (Freud 1919/1985: 345) in not just the protagonists of the story, who find themselves at the centre of a terrifying maelstrom, but also the audience, whose exposure to these horrors they must also comprehend. Sigmund Freud identified the 'uncanny' (or the German *unheimlich*, which translates as 'unhomely') as 'that class of the frightening which leads back to what is known of old and long familiar [but] something has to be added to what is novel and unfamiliar in order to make it uncanny' (Freud 1919/1985: 341). Freud quotes the nineteenth-century German philosopher Friedrich Wilhelm Joseph Schelling in his 1919 essay on the concept of the uncanny: '*Unheimlich* is the name for everything that ought to have remained... secret and hidden but has come to light' (Freud 1919/1985: 345).

The Gothic novel concerns itself with strange yet simultaneously familiar environments which become instilled with a sense of dread and horror – for example, think of the titular fortress in Horace Walpole's *The Castle of Otranto* (1764), the very first Gothic novel, and Ann Radcliffe's *The Mysteries of Udolpho* (1794), whose Count Montoni, the splendid, red-eyed, archetypal Gothic villain, imprisons the affectionate heroine Emily in a potentially haunted French castle. Late-period Gothics from the Victorian era attach great importance to specific locations which again are intended to bring fear and dread to the participant or reader: Charlotte Brontë's *Jane Eyre* (1847), with its mysterious attic room at Thornfield Hall, and Castle Dracula in Bram Stoker's *Dracula* (1897). As the increasingly anxious solicitor Jonathan Harker explores the great castle, Stoker describes the 'prison' (for that is what it has become to Harker) as follows:

> The castle was built on the corner of a great rock, so that on three sides it was quite impregnable, and great windows were placed here where sling, or bow, or culverin

> could not reach, and consequently light and comfort, impossible to a position which had to be guarded, were secured. The windows were curtainless, and the yellow moonlight, flooding in through the diamond panes, enabled one to see even colours, whilst it softened the wealth of dust which lay over all and disguised in some measure the ravages of time and the moth. My lamp seemed to be of little effect in the brilliant moonlight, but I was glad to have it with me, for there was a dread loneliness in the place which chilled my heart and made my nerves tremble. Still, it was better than living alone in the rooms which I had come to hate from the presence of the Count, and after trying a little to school my nerves, I found a soft quietude come over me. (Stoker 1897/1965: 37)

These are 'Bad Places', an idea which Stephen King discusses at length in *Danse Macabre*, his superb 1981 study of the horror genre across cinema, literature, comic books and radio:

> It doesn't hurt to emphasise again that horror fiction is a cold touch in the midst of the familiar, and good horror fiction applies this cold touch with sudden, unexpected pressure. When we go home and shoot the bolt on the door, we like to think we're locking trouble out. The good horror story about the Bad Place whispers that we are not locking the world out; we are locking ourselves in... with *them*. (King 1981: 299)

Fig. 13 *The Bad Place.*

The cabin in the woods in *The Evil Dead* is one such example of a 'bad' or 'horrible' place, where awful secrets lay hidden or where terrors lurk within the walls, waiting to be unleashed upon unsuspecting owners or visitors to these cursed dwellings. Haunted house stories focus exclusively on the Bad Place ('A house with an unsavoury history,' writes King [1981: 300]), but they appear everywhere in the genre: Roderick Usher's mansion in Edgar Allan Poe's 1839 short story *The Fall of the House of Usher* and the various film versions, the most important being Roger Corman's 1960 film *House of Usher*, the first in his eight-film Poe series; James Whale's *The Old Dark House* (1932), from J.B. Priestley's 1927 novel *Benighted*; the four film adaptations – 1927, 1930 (as *The Cat Creeps*), 1939 and 1977 – of John Willard's 1922 stage play *The Cat and the Canary*; Robert Siodmak (1945) and Peter Collinson's (1974) *The Spiral Staircase*, from the novel *Some Must Watch* (1933) by Ethel Lina White; Alfred Hitchcock's *Psycho* (1960), based on Robert Bloch's novel of 1959, the Bates Motel being one of the genre's quintessential Bad Places; Henry James' 1898 novella *The Turn of the Screw* and its 1961 film adaptation by Jack Cardiff, *The Innocents*; Robert Wise's *The Haunting*, the outstanding 1963 version of Shirley Jackson's *The Haunting of Hill House*, Jackson's 1959 novel, along with Anne Rivers Siddons' *The House Next Door* (1978), remaining the most pertinent literary examples of the Bad Place concept; Stuart Rosenberg's *The Amityville Horror* (1979), an adaptation of Jay Anson's 'true fiction' novel (1977) and one of the most commercially successful of the Bad Place movies; and the novel (Stephen King, 1977), film (Stanley Kubrick, 1980) and, later, television series (1997) of *The Shining*, with its isolated, ghost-inhabited Overlook Hotel. Also prior to *The Evil Dead*, genuinely frightening Bad Places proliferated on TV, in particular the bayou mansion in *Pigeons from Hell*, a 1961 episode of *Thriller*, directed by John Newland from a 1934 story by Robert E. Howard; the cottage in Don Taylor's *The Exorcism*, one of only three surviving episodes of the short-lived BBC series *Dead of Night* (1972); and the Marsten House in Tobe Hooper's 1979 adaptation of King's novel *'Salem's Lot*, which recalls the decaying motel and farmhouse in Hooper's earlier *Eaten Alive* (1976) and *The Texas Chainsaw Massacre*.

The Bad Place cannot be confined to medieval castles, old dark houses and sinister hotels, but can manifest itself in a number of different forms; in fact a whole variety of locations which, referring back to Freud's theory of the uncanny, are transformed into sites of terror: carnivals (Herk Harvey's *Carnival of Souls*, 1962), schools (Renee Daalder's

Massacre at Central High, 1976), forests (Charles B. Pierce's *The Legend of Boggy Creek*, 1972), summer camps (Sean S. Cunningham's *Friday the 13th*), boats (Vernon Sewell's *Ghost Ship*, 1952), islands (Robin Hardy's *The Wicker Man*, 1973), trains (Eugenio Martin's *Horror Express / Panico en el Transiberiano*, 1972), lighthouses (John Carpenter's *The Fog*, 1979), shopping malls (George A. Romero's *Dawn of the Dead*), jungles (Ruggero Deodato's *Cannibal Holocaust*, 1979), museums (Andre DeToth's *House of Wax*, 1953), the ocean (Steven Spielberg's *Jaws*, 1975), cars (Carpenter's *Christine*, 1983), cinemas (Lamberto Bava's *Demons / Dèmoni*, 1985), dance schools (Dario Argento's *Suspiria*, 1976), apartment blocks (David Cronenberg's *Shivers / The Parasite Murders*, 1974), hotels (Lucio Fulci's *The Beyond / ... E tu vivrai nel terrore! L'Aldila*, 1981), theatres (Pete Walker's *The Flesh and Blood Show*, 1972), pubs (Sidney Hayers' *Revenge*, 1971), circuses (Tod Browning's *Freaks*, 1932) and mines (John Gilling's *The Plague of the Zombies*, 1966).[1]

Fig. 14 The Bates residence in Psycho.

THE BAD DREAM

Like many of the successful films that followed, *Night of the Living Dead* adopts the logic of the nightmare, the sensation that, no matter how you run, you'll never get away from the monster behind you. Unity of space and time is a necessary underpinning for the bad dream, and *Night of the Living Dead* – like *The Texas*

Chainsaw Massacre, *The Hills Have Eyes*, *Halloween* and *The Evil Dead* – takes place in a limited area during a single night. (Newman 1988/2011: 12/13)

The Evil Dead is one of a number of horror movies – from James Whale's *The Old Dark House* through to Alfred Hitchcock's *The Birds* (1963, from Daphne du Maurier's 1952 tale) and *Night of the Living Dead*, and on towards seminal 1970s horrors such as *The Texas Chainsaw Massacre*, *The Hills Have Eyes* and *Halloween* – which locate their nightmares in one location (a small town, a farmhouse, a desert outpost, etc.) in a time frame of 24–48 hours. This compactness allows for an increase in tension and claustrophobia. The remoteness of the cabin (as with the farmhouse and desert dwellings depicted in *Night of the Living Dead*, *The Texas Chainsaw Massacre* and *The Hills Have Eyes*) prolongs the agony for the protagonists as there is no escape from the terrors that surround them. The nightmare is never-ending, and refuge is impossible as, in *The Evil Dead*, even the woods are alive with demonic trees and other restless evils.

So how does the structure of *The Evil Dead* create a Bad Dream effect? Nightmares are transient, often lucid, frightening imagery drawn from our subconscious and not always open to straightforward interpretation. The waking nightmares in which the characters of the three movies most closely aligned to *The Evil Dead* – Ben and Barbra, in particular, in *Night of the Living Dead*, Sally and Franklin in *The Texas Chainsaw Massacre*, the Carter family in *The Hills Have Eyes* – find themselves ensnared are ephemeral in that they are temporally restrictive; the horrors which confront them, however, are extensive, bewildering, and ultimately tragic.

Like the Western, horror cinema often functions as a three-act play. An interesting example of this approach would be the Hammer Dracula films of the 1960s and 1970s:

- Act One: Count Dracula's remains – ashes (Terence Fisher's *Dracula, Prince of Darkness*, 1965; Alan Gibson's *Dracula A.D. 1972*, 1972), blood (Peter Sasdy's *Taste the Blood of Dracula*, 1969) or, as in Freddie Francis' *Dracula Has Risen from the Grave* (1968), his entire body faithfully preserved in ice – are located and he is duly resurrected (sometimes intentionally by minions, at other times by accident).

- Act Two: The Count seeks revenge upon those responsible for his unwanted revivification through the traditional vampirisation process (in *Taste the Blood of Dracula* it's the teenage children, under Dracula's spell, who exact the revenge).

- Act Three: The Count is hunted down by the hero or heroes and destroyed in one of a number of disparate ways: water (*Dracula, Prince of Darkness*), impalement (*Dracula Has Risen from the Grave*), fire (Roy Ward Baker's *Scars of Dracula*, 1970) and, most unusually, a hawthorn bush (Gibson's *The Satanic Rites of Dracula*, 1973).

The Evil Dead also conforms to the three-act strategy, but in a weird and wonderful way. In Act One, the characters arrive at the cabin and the demons are called forth. Act Two centres on the havoc created by the possession, one by one, of each member of the group. With only a battered and bloodied Ash left alive, Act Three is unresolved and, by following the 'logic' of a nightmare, the terrors continue. What at first appears to constitute closure (Ash 'awakens' from the Bad Dream as the sun rises over the forest) is merely a foretaste of suggested horrors to come as the Force descends upon him as he stands desolate outside the cabin.

The opening of the film juxtaposes scenes of Ash, Linda and the others driving along the mountain roads (the two fishermen they pass are played by Sam Raimi and Rob Tapert) to what will be their final destination with shots from the POV of the Force prowling through the woods. Immediately there is a connection established between our group and this unseen presence – do these scenes suggest that the Force is already at work, perhaps manipulating events (the near-miss with the pick-up truck, the perilous crossing of the bridge, the unexplained destruction of the same bridge later in the film)?

A low-level shot of Scott walking towards the cabin mirrors a similar scene in *The Texas Chainsaw Massacre* of Pam (Teri McMinn) approaching the Sawyer family farmhouse. Externally the cabin is the more mysterious of the two, but both abodes are in visible decline. In keeping with horror movie convention, the cabin in the woods is quite clearly signposted as a 'bad' or 'horrible' place from its very first appearance. The camera follows Scott as he approaches the front porch, the cabin looming towards him in a sinisterly fashion. The Force also seems to have control over the porch swing, as it ceases to rock from side to side when Scott takes down the key from the door ledge. What is homely and familiar is now strange and menacing, and there are other such examples later in the film. An adjacent tool shed is reminiscent of the abattoir-like Sawyer house interior: hooks, chains, various hand tools, but also animal, bird and fish bones are strung from the roof beams.

Fig. 15 Time stands still as the nightmare starts.

The cabin's main room is more welcoming once the group unpack, but as evening draws in the Force becomes more malignant. The first indication of this occurs in the sequence involving Cheryl, the clock and the sketch pad. The clock's pendulum stops suddenly at eight minutes to six. Voices can be heard whispering from beyond the open window ('Join us... join us...'). The Bad Dream construction of *The Evil Dead* locates its inescapable terrors in a dusk-till-dawn timeframe, which is compact and undeniably effective. As the curtains billow, the pencil in Cheryl's hand uncontrollably draws jagged lines on the pad, tearing the paper as it does so. A face of some kind is revealed to have been crudely sketched; a close-up of this 'face' as she lowers the pad shows the cellar trapdoor jerking upwards a few times before settling to rest. Has the Force already chosen Cheryl as the primary host for the spirits which are soon to be set free? After all, it's her unforgettably demonic visage which will be later peering up through the trapdoor. This sequence represents the first real indication to character and audience that the cabin is a truly Bad Place. The fact that Cheryl does not appear to speak about her strange experience with the others in the group suggests that the Force has taken latent possession of the woman well before the demons have been violently released.

However, before long the group will all be made aware of just how unusual the cabin actually is. At dinner, the trapdoor suddenly flings itself open and they gather around the cellar entrance before Scott, then Ash, decide to venture down the staircase into the dark space below. Cellars are a horror movie staple, always cold, dank and full of shadows, and *The Evil Dead*'s cellar conforms precisely to this cliché. Following Scott, Ash's lamp casts its glow upon a door at the other end, which reveals Scott and his discovery of the shotgun and tape recorder, not to mention a torn cinema poster of *The Hills Have Eyes*, a reference to both the influence of Wes Craven's film and the similarly ripped poster for Steven Spielberg's *Jaws* which can be glimpsed briefly in *The Hills Have Eyes* (Craven would repay the compliment by featuring scenes from *The Evil Dead* playing on television in *A Nightmare on Elm Street*, 1984). It's in this room that Ash discovers the strange book (one of the illustrations bears a resemblance to the 'face' which Cheryl scrawls on the sketch pad) and the skull-hilted dagger.

The group listen intently, if confusedly, to the voice on the tape recorder as a storm breaks out and lightning flashes across the night sky. Raimi doesn't seem overly concerned about the generic clichés in these early scenes, as the films which he and his key collaborators acknowledge as inspiring *The Evil Dead* toy with and then subvert horror conventions. Raimi's film does likewise, especially in its depiction of Ash as a wide-eyed scaredy-cat who only gets his act together when the going gets really tough.

The next sequence is one of the most visually striking in the film, a credit to Raimi that he had the rather precocious ability to create such a dramatic *mise-en-scène* with his meagre resources. As the professor's incantations are heard on the tape, the earth outside the cabin splits apart to reveal a glowing red furnace; meanwhile inside Cheryl screams for the tape to be shut off before a tree branch crashes through one of the windows. Raimi's use of framing is superb; in particular, the low-angle exterior shot with the foregrounded earth appearing to bubble open as the demonic spirits are resurrected while in the near distance the cabin awaits their visitation, and the following scene where Cheryl sits huddled in front of the tape recorder in medium shot, as over her right shoulder darkness slowly falls across the light illuminating the cabin from outside the window. Special mention must be made to Edna Ruth Paul, the film's editor, whose work is exceptional throughout the movie, and helps to sandpaper some of the rougher edges. Interesting sidenote: Paul's assistant was Joel Coen, whose directorial debut, 1983's *Blood Simple*, displays much of the bravura enthusiasm of *The Evil Dead*. His brother Ethan contributed to the professor's narration (spoken by Bob Dorian) heard on the tape recording. Like Raimi, the Coens are now firmly established in the Hollywood mainstream.

The tree rape, and the scenes which lead directly to it, convey through music and sound effects a genuinely nightmarish atmosphere. Upon becoming aware of a noise outside the cabin, Cheryl unwisely steps into the cold, misty forest. 'I know someone's out there... I heard you, I heard you in the cellar,' she calls to whatever may be lurking behind any one of a thousand trees. Branches are heard being broken somewhere close by, strange noises fill the air, and the Force begins to advance towards her, cutting through the trees and branches which obstruct its path. Vines seize Cheryl by her thighs, tightening themselves around her legs, wrists and neck, and tearing at her bathrobe before unbalancing her, causing Cheryl to fall backwards where the vines strap her to the ground, rip her undershirt and proceed to 'rape' her. With the exception of one brief flash of Ellen Sandweiss' left breast the sexual violation is suggested largely through the actresses' screams and facial expressions and reverse printing, although the shot of one huge vine thudding into her crotch provides a jolting awareness of what the vines intend to do with Cheryl now that she has been lured away from the cabin.

Does this sequence represent a misogynistic attitude on the part of its makers? Do the Renaissance members harbour distrustful feelings towards women, especially as all three of the female characters succumb to possession and dismemberment? The director has subsequently felt uncomfortable enough to express misgivings about shooting the scene. However, the tree rape functions contextually as just one example of the film's 'illogical' dream-logic; anything can happen in this universe, Sam Raimi seems to be telling us, even a shocking sexual assault by something as ridiculous as a plant. Jake Horsley describes the scene most eloquently in his book *The Blood Poets*: '[the scene] is genuinely imaginative, a borderline artistic-mythic concept. Those pagan roots have emerged again and dragged the maiden, like Persephone into Hades, back to the jungle' (Horsley 1999: 248).

After she succeeds in breaking free of her bonds, Cheryl's frantic run through the forest pursued by the Force is reminiscent of Leatherface's woodland chase after Sally in *The Texas Chainsaw Massacre*. Although Leatherface is a more tangible, physical threat, the Force is the more menacing of the two pursuers as neither Cheryl nor the audience knows precisely what it is that can move at frightening speed and cause trees to tumble in its path. Once again, the editing is exemplary, and Raimi skilfully combines POV shots of the Force with tight close-ups of Cheryl's face and legs and frenetic camera movements as it follows, tracks and even precedes her until she finally reaches the cabin and the Force eventually retreats with a disappointed yet humorous groan.

Another scene of superb spookiness occurs soon after. Ash agrees to drive Cheryl back to town but, sensing that there is something up ahead in the murky distance, Ash stops the car to investigate. The camera tilts as Cheryl decides to follow, adding to the realisation that what they are now experiencing is somewhat off-kilter. POV shots (this time from Cheryl's not the Force's perspective) and false scares (a branch falling in front of Cheryl) add to the tension of the scene. Creaking and wailing noises can be heard, and Joe DeLuca's score is at its most creepily effective here; DeLuca draws considerable inspiration from the work of Bernard Herrmann, whose screeching strings for *Psycho* and moody, sinister score for Martin Scorsese's *Taxi Driver* (1976) have been much imitated. Cheryl advances through the fog towards what remains of the bridge they crossed earlier that afternoon, its girders twisted into the shape of a claw.

Crucially, only Ash is aware of how to dispose of the demons which are soon to possess his friends. Listening through an earpiece so as not to disturb the others, he hears the professor explain that bodily dismemberment is the only way to bring to an end the possessed state of those cursed by the demons in the Book. From this point on, the horrors multiply at a frantic pace. The transformation of Cheryl during the playing card game is arguably the film's most frightening sequence – it moves from playfulness and joviality to wide-eyed terror in the space of seconds. It's quite a shock when Cheryl, sitting quietly at the window, correctly calls the cards which Linda and Shelly are holding, and when she suddenly spins her head towards the others with a face like Regan MacNeil's big sister, we know that the rollercoaster is completely out of control. 'Why have you disturbed our sleep?' Cheryl says with a voice which echoes from beyond the grave. 'Awakened us from our ancient slumbers? You will die like the others before you. One by one we will take you.' Cheryl levitates as she speaks, the cabin appearing to grow darker before she falls to the floor, seemingly unconscious. As she jerks awake she stabs Linda in the ankle with a pencil; the twisting, screaming, and oozing blood makes this scene almost unbearable to watch, it feels more excruciatingly real and painful than the over-the-top, comic book gore which soon follows.

In terms of *The Evil Dead*'s unremitting gruesomeness, it's impossible to underestimate the influence of the EC comics of the 1950s. Published by William M. Gaines between 1950 and 1954, the EC titles (*The Haunt of Fear*, *Tales from the Crypt*, *The Vault of Horror*, *Crime SuspensStories*, *Shock SuspensStories*, *Weird Fantasy* and *Weird Science*) created such an impact that conservative moral values were considered to be threatened and undermined in a manner not unlike the 'video nasty' hysteria in Britain in the 1980s (see Chapter 5). The comics were denounced as being the root cause of juvenile delinquency in America, with psychologist Fredric Wertham's best-selling study of the subject, *Seduction of the Innocent* (1954), effectively ending the publication of horror comics in the United States for the next two decades. EC comics (particularly *The Haunt of Fear*, *Tales from the Crypt* and *The Vault of Horror*) are characterised by a dark moral code, an emphasis on crudeness over subtlety, and the vivid illustrations of artists such as Johnny Craig.

From here on in *The Evil Dead* becomes an eye-popping exercise in absurd, wild shock-horror, barely pausing for breath as it launches an aural and visual sensory assault. Scott manages to kick the violently possessed Cheryl backwards into the cellar and secures it sufficiently to prevent her/it from breaking out. The POV shots of Cheryl peering up through the trapdoor (as with those of the Force, the vines and unknown things in the woods) are effectively staged, and give a very real sense of just how small the cabin actually is. As Shelly enters one of the bedrooms the Force bursts through the window. It's her boyfriend Scott who investigates, not Ash, who appears oblivious to the sound of Shelly's screaming and the crashing window; at this point in the movie Scott is the more assertive of the male characters and the one most likely to secure a safe passage for the others in the group. Ash is only jolted into action when his friend is attacked by the now-possessed Shelly, although she hurls him into a bookcase before attempting to stab Scott with the Kandarian dagger. Shelly's unearthly cries of 'Join us', coupled with Cheryl's desperate rattling of the trapdoor chains, her eyes blazing and with blood bubbling from her mouth, are genuinely disconcerting. Scott uses his own knife to sever Shelly's hand and she finishes the job herself by permanently detaching the limb with her teeth (although Bruce Campbell and Richard DeManincor's facial expressions as they watch with disgust the scene unfolding before them might be considered amateurish they are entirely appropriate to the bizarre comic-strip orchestrations of the film's second half).

As if to reinforce its EC credentials the film's set-pieces become increasingly outlandish. A fine example is Shelly's demise: Scott picks up the blood-drenched dagger and thrusts it into her back. With Shelly's severed hand still attached it gives the impression that she is actually stabbing herself. She screams in agony and the skull-decorated hilt begins to smoulder and ooze blood. She falls to the cabin floor and all kinds of fluids burst from her writhing body until she rises up again and advances upon Ash and Scott. Ash, clutching an axe, cringes near the window, leaving Scott to wrench it from his hands and dismember Shelly. The floor and walls become awash with blood and the various limbs (head, arms, legs, feet) continue to twitch. After they bury the body parts in a shallow grave, Scott decides to abandon Ash and Linda, whom Ash has put to bed following her attack by the possessed Cheryl. Checking on her as she sleeps, Ash observes the wound on her ankle suddenly turn into something resembling a spider's web. With a hideous, Gwynplaine-like grin on her face and her eyes milky white, the now-possessed Linda forces Ash to back off down the hallway where he encounters Scott, who has just been attacked by something in the woods. Linda's possessed state is significantly different from that of Cheryl and Shelly: her face could almost pass for normal were it not for the eyes, but her voice is child-like and she giggles constantly. Her behaviour is less physically threatening than the others but at the same time less predictable and more insinuating. Linda continues to laugh at Ash even after he's punched her three times in the face. When Ash points the shotgun at her Linda raises her head and appears to have reverted back to her human state; Cheryl, too, calls out that she's okay, but as he attempts to unlock the chains securing the trapdoor she reaches up and clutches at his throat. Breaking loose, he sees that Linda is possessed again. 'We're going to get you,' she sings in a nursery-rhyme fashion before stabbing him in the arm with the same dagger which was used to despatch Shelly earlier. Like Shelly, Linda is stabbed in the back, causing blood and white fluid to spew from her mouth and an enraged Cheryl to pound on the trapdoor. Fastening her to the work bench in the tool shed, Ash is about to use a chainsaw to dismember Linda but is unable to do so when he notices the chain around her neck, a silver magnifying glass which he had given to her earlier that night as token of his love. Instead, he decides to bury her next to Shelly but as he digs the hole Linda is reanimated as Cheryl finally succeeds in breaking out of the cellar (in an effective series of close cross-cuts between the hinges of the trapdoor snapping, Linda's

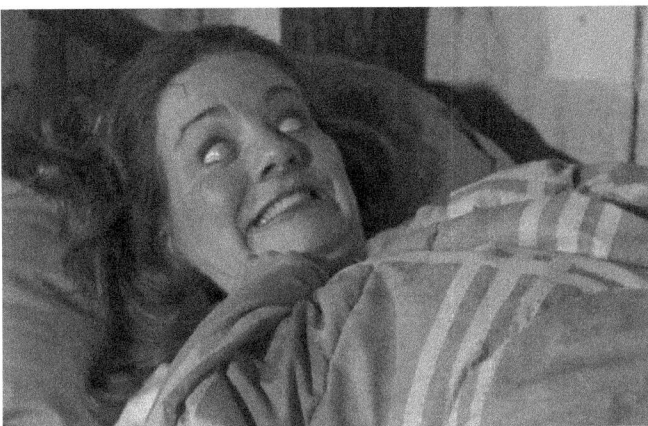

Fig. 16 Possessed Linda.

white eyes reopening and a POV shot from within the grave as Ash shovels dirt into the hole).

There then follows a resurrection sequence which is as effective as the nightmarish graveyard scenes in John Gilling's *The Plague of the Zombies*, Bob Clark's *Children Shouldn't Play With Dead Things* (1972) and Lucio Fulci's *Zombie Flesh Eaters* (*Zombi 2*, 1979): Linda's hand reaches upwards and snatches Ash's ankle before she rises up out of the earth, scratching horribly at his leg (the actress playing Linda here is actually Cheryl Guttridge, who 'Fake Shemps' extensively throughout the film, her demonic make-up resembling her namesake in the cabin cellar). Ash beats the cackling Linda with a plank before decapitating her with the spade he used to dig her grave. Low angle shots are used extremely well in *The Evil Dead* and this sequence is one of the best: first a shot from Ash's POV as he looks up and sees Linda leaping into the air above him, cutting to another low shot as he swings the spade, a close-up as he severs her head, the spade following through, Linda's head spinning in the air and hurtling towards the camera, a shot of blood spurting from her neck, an extreme close-up of Ash's wild eyes, the screen filling with blood as her headless torso topples towards the prostrate Ash, and a horrible yet funny shot of Linda's severed head landing with a plop in the foreground as her body lands on top of Ash in the background. His face is sprayed with blood from Linda's neck while she straddles him, her head continuing to laugh. It's a wonderfully

Fig. 17 Ash prepares to bury Linda.

ridiculous sequence, frightening, gruesome and funny all at once and it encapsulates so much of why *The Evil Dead* caught the imagination of horror fans in the 1980s and continues to do so well into the twenty-first century.

Upon returning to the cabin Ash finds the cellar trapdoor open and Cheryl missing. Grabbing the shotgun Ash follows a noise in one of the bedrooms but as he points the gun at the shower curtain Cheryl lunges at him from the open window. Although Ash shoots her in the throat Cheryl continues to advance towards him. Tim Philo's frantic camera follows him as he closes as many doors as he can to keep Cheryl out but, realising that he needs more shotgun shells, he ventures down into the cellar, only to be drenched with blood which inexplicably bursts from an overhead water pipe (one of the mad, illogical scenes which *The Evil Dead* revels in). Plug sockets drip blood, so do the walls (shades of Stuart Rosenberg's *The Amityville Horror*), a lightbulb fills up with the red stuff (a direct reference to one of Raimi's favourite Three Stooges shorts, Del Lord's 1940 *A Plumbing We Will Go*, although in that film it's water not blood), a vintage record player (the wind-up variety dating back to the 1930s) turns itself on, and so does a cine-projector, which clicks into life and captures Ash in its beam as blood runs down the screen and drips onto the lens. It quickly catches fire and explodes, the lightbulb bursts and the gramophone winds down, the cellar floor becoming filled with puddles of blood. Back upstairs the clock's hands spin crazily (there's even a shot from the clock's

Fig. 18 Linda rises from the grave.

POV before the hands settle to rest again at ten minutes to six). The next sequence features a number of disorientating camera angles as first the camera rises from a low off-kilter position and pans from left to right as Ash walks across the cabin floor. An upside-down overhead shot (Raimi himself is holding the camera on this one, hanging from the rafters) observes Ash from behind walking towards the fireplace before the camera tilts downwards and then up again, Ash's face looming into view and pulling back as he looks fearfully over his shoulders. It's a testament to Raimi's prodigious talent as a filmmaker, and it takes considerable ingenuity to create narrative tension simply by imaginatively locating the camera in unusual positions, especially given the inhospitable working conditions.

The shutters begin to flap uncontrollably and there are more high-angle shots from the ceiling as Ash walks the floor. In homage to Jean Cocteau's *Orphée* (*Orpheus*, 1950), Ash looks at himself in a mirror and reaches out towards his reflection, his hand connecting with the surface to reveal that it's water (in Cocteau's masterpiece a mirror serves as the gateway to another world). Ash lets out a scream and fires a shot at a dark shape which passes the window before Cheryl's arms burst through the door he is leaning against and seize his neck and face. 'Join us,' she implores again but he breaks free, fires a shot at her and attempts to barricade the door. Scott, now in the full throes of demonic possession, sits bolt upright and lunges at Ash, lifting him up off the ground. In one of the film's most shocking moments Ash gouges out Scott's eyes in close-up, blood pouring from the sockets. He extracts a piece of wood protruding from Scott's stomach and blood bursts out in waterfall fashion. As Cheryl breaks down the door, Ash notices the Book of the Dead next to the fireplace but before he can lay his hands upon it, Cheryl knocks him to the floor. Ash crawls towards the Book but the now-smouldering Scott pulls him back and Cheryl beats him with a poker; however, he uses Linda's necklace (which he had dropped after taking it from his pocket earlier) to hook the evil document, which has already begun to catch light, and drag it towards him. He picks it up and hurls it into the blazing fire.

What follows next is the film's stand-out sequence. Make-up artist Tom Sullivan may have been inspired by the dissolve-into-dust finale of Terence Fisher's *Dracula* (*Horror of Dracula*, 1958) but the meltdowns bear more of a resemblance to the conclusion of Robert Fuest's *The Devil's Rain* (1975), in which Ernest Borgnine's Satanic followers are reduced to goo. However, Raimi's demon disintegrations are far more extravagant. Cheryl stops beating Ash and the poker falls from her hand, her face begins to crack open and her hair falls out, the bones crumble, the skin stretches and turns blue, and a huge claw bursts from her stomach and back. As her head caves in it reveals a screaming skull. Scott's body twitches and his bones also begin to crumble. Blood and all manner of coloured liquids ooze from his skull, a green puke-like substance flows and claws erupt from his back, maggots and cockroaches crawl. Even the face on the cover of the Book starts to melt, sticking out its tongue in a snake-like fashion.

'Join us,' commands a booming voice, but it fades away. As dawn breaks Ash leaves the cabin and walks outside. A close-up of the leafy ground suddenly turns into the familiar POV of the Force; the invisible demon races through the rear entrance of the cabin, into the main room and out of the front door. Ash screams as he turns his face towards the camera.

By taking what is familiar and natural (forest, log cabin, clock, necklace) and adding something unnatural to it (the sudden stopping of the clock, which announces the presence to the characters of a malevolent force), *The Evil Dead* succeeds in generating a 'bad dream' effect with the cabin clearly marked out as a 'bad place' even before the evil spirits are unleashed. Several elements are combined almost perfectly to create this effect: the photography by Tim Philo, in particular, effectively generates an atmosphere of dread by utilising a mixture of camera angles (low shots, extreme close-ups, high angle shots) and an especially fervent use of the subjective camera technique. It isn't just the characters or the ever-present Force from whose position we view the action but inanimate objects too (the cabin clock, for example, or the trees). Tight close-ups help to develop a sense of claustrophobia, that the characters are trapped within the confines of this horrible place while time literally stands still and the bad dream becomes increasingly hellish (the nightmare carries on even after the spell appears to have been broken).

The Evil Dead is undoubtedly a violent film but its gross-out splatter is exaggerated and used for darkly comical effect. The make-up effects, music, editing and sound design (by Joseph R. Masefield, John Mason, Josh Becker and Mel Zelniker) are crucial to establishing the strange mood and scary atmospherics which helped turn *The Evil Dead* into the low-budget success story of the early 1980s.

Notes

1. Bad Places also figure prominently in such films as Edgar G. Ulmer's *The Black Cat* (1934), the expressionist mansion belonging to Hjalamar Poelzig (Boris Karloff) having been erected on the site of a mass World War I grave; Roy William Neill's underrated *The Black Room* (1935); George Marshall's *The Ghost Breakers* (1940), a close relative of *The Cat and the Canary*, from a play by Paul Dickey and Charles W. Goddard; Lewis Allen's *The Uninvited* (1944); William Castle's *House on Haunted Hill* (1958), with its floating skeletons and severed heads; Robert Hartford-Davis' Donald and Derek Ford-scripted Gothic *The Black Torment* (1964); David Greene's *The Shuttered Room* (1966), from a story (1959) by H.P. Lovecraft and August Derleth (one of Derleth's many posthumous 'collaborations' with Lovecraft); John Hough's *The Legend of Hell House* (1973), scripted by Richard Matheson from his 1971 novel *Hell House*; *Burnt Offerings* (1976), Dan Curtis' film of Robert Marasco's 1973 novel; and Charles B. Pierce's fun *The Evictors* (1979).

Chapter 4: Ash as the 'Final Girl'

Fig. 19 Jamie Lee Curtis as Laurie in Halloween.

In her ground-breaking 1992 study of gender politics in the modern horror film, *Men, Women and Chainsaws*, Carol J. Clover acutely identifies a cinematic plot device she terms the 'Final Girl':

> The image of the distressed female most likely to linger in memory is the image of the one who did not die: the survivor, or Final Girl. She is the one who encounters the mutilated bodies of her friends and perceives the full extent of the preceding horror and of her own peril; who is chased, cornered, wounded; whom we see scream, stagger, fall, rise, and scream again. She is abject terror personified. If her friends knew they were about to die only seconds before the event, the Final Girl lives with the knowledge for long minutes or hours. She alone looks death in the face, but she alone also finds the strength either to stay the killer long enough to be rescued (ending A) or to kill him herself (ending B). But in either case, from 1974 on, the survivor figure has been female. In [William] Schoell's words [in his 1985 book *Stay Out of the Shower: Twenty-Five Years of Shocking Films Beginning With 'Psycho'*]: 'The vast majority of contemporary shockers, whether in the sexist mold or not, feature climaxes in which the women fight back against their attackers – the wandering, humourless psychos who populate these films. They often show more courage and levelheadedness than their cringing male counterparts'. Her scene occupies the last ten to twenty minutes (thirty in the case of *Texas Chain Saw I*) and contains the film's emphatic climax. (Clover 1992: 35-36)

The most famous, and also the most definitive, examples of Clover's Final Girl theory can be found in the classics of the 1970s American horror film: in John Carpenter's *Halloween* Clover considers babysitter Laurie Strode (Jamie Lee Curtis) to be 'the original Final Girl' (Clover 1992: 232). Not only does she survive the slaughter of her friends Annie (Nancy Loomis), Lynda (P.J. Soles) and Bob (John Michael Graham) but she retaliates with keen awareness and bravery as escaped lunatic Michael Myers (played both by Nick Castle and, at the very end of the film, by Tony Moran) descends upon not only her but her two charges, Lindsey (Kyle Richards) and Tommy (Brian Andrews). Using a clothes hanger as a weapon, she succeeds in stabbing Michael in the eye but even a last-minute intervention from his psychiatrist, Dr. Loomis (Donald Pleasence), who shoots him several times causing Michael to fall out of the bedroom window, isn't enough to stop the mad killer. Michael vanishes, only to reappear as an even more indestructible bogeyman in Rick Rosenthal's Carpenter-scripted *Halloween II* (1981, which has the feel of an imitation rather than a legitimate sequel, but adds gravitas to Curtis' Final Girl by revealing that she is in fact Michael's sister). Later sequels – Dwight H. Little's *Halloween 4: The Return of Michael Myers* (1988), Dominique Othenin-Girard's *Halloween 5: The Revenge of Michael Myers* (1989) and Joe Chappelle's *Halloween 6: The Curse of Michael Myers* (1995) – focus on Loomis' tireless efforts to put an end to Michael's incessant killing spree. Steve Miner's *Halloween H20: 20 Years Later* (1998), Rosenthal's *Halloween: Resurrection* (2002) and David Gordon Green's 2018 re-boot bring back Curtis as Laurie for encores. Rob Zombie's remakes of *Halloween* (2007) and *Halloween II* (2009) are negligible in their attitude towards the Final Girl, with greater emphasis placed on Michael's troubled background and the director's misanthropic worldview, and the films are distinguished solely by the quality of their supporting casts (Brad Dourif, Ken Foree, Sid Haig, Danielle Harris, Margot Kidder, Udo Kier, Richard Lynch, Malcolm McDowell, Danny Trejo, Dee Wallace). Tommy Lee Wallace's *Halloween III: Season of the Witch* (1982) ignores the previous two films in the cycle but remains an interesting aberration, its commercial failure sadly preventing further explorations on subjects based on All Hallows' Eve.

Fig. 20 Marilyn Burns as Sally in The Texas Chainsaw Massacre.

Tobe Hooper's seminal, nightmarish *The Texas Chainsaw Massacre* set the standard for the Final Girl movie. Sally Hardesty (Marilyn Burns), her wheelchair-bound brother Franklin (Paul A. Partain) and friends Jerry (Allen Danziger), Kirk (William Vail) and Pam (Teri McMinn), are attacked by a family of crazed cannibals in rural Texas. Sally survives, but not before being captured, tortured and pursued by the chainsaw-wielding Leatherface (Gunnar Hansen). Sally's instincts are driven by a desperate need for survival, but in Hooper's demented 1986 sequel *The Texas Chainsaw Massacre 2*, disc jockey Vanita 'Stretch' Brock (Caroline Williams) displays a propensity for self-defence rather than self-preservation. The tone has changed dramatically, from grim, unrelenting horror in the first film to wild, over-the-top gore (in stark contrast to the 1974 film, which cuts away from the chainsaw mutilations and allows the claustrophobic atmosphere, piercing screams and unusual sound effects to create the maximum impact). Further sequels/remakes – Jeff Burr's *Leatherface: The Texas Chainsaw Massacre III* (1989), *The Return of the Texas Chainsaw Massacre* (1994, directed by Kim Henkel, co-writer of the first film), Marcus Nispel's *The Texas Chainsaw Massacre* (2003), Jonathan Liebesman's *The Texas Chainsaw Massacre: The Beginning* (2006), John Luessenhop's *Texas Chainsaw 3D* (2012) and Julien Maury and Alexandre Bustillo's *Leatherface* (2017) – feature their own Final Girls with varying degrees of success (Alexandra Daddario as Heather generates a fair amount of empathy in *Texas Chainsaw 3D*).

Fig. 21 Camille Keaton as Jennifer in I Spit on Your Grave.

Less reputable, but no less interesting and far nastier than either *The Texas Chainsaw Massacre* or *Halloween* is Meir Zarchi's *I Spit on Your Grave* (1978), a rape-revenge shocker originally titled *Day of the Woman*, which features Camille Keaton as Jennifer, a New York writer who decides to spend the summer at a country retreat to finish a novel only to be first terrorised and then beaten and savagely raped by a gang of locals, Johnny (Eron Tabor), Matthew (Richard Pace), Stanley (Anthony Nichols) and Andy (Gunter Kleemann). Having instructed Matthew, the most impressionable of the group, to dispatch the girl with a knife once they are through with her, he instead takes sympathy on Jennifer (he'd taken a shine to her during one of the film's more innocent early scenes) and allows her to live, unbeknownst to the others in the group. Jennifer re-emerges as an angel of vengeance, asking for forgiveness in a local church before embarking on a violent killing spree in which her assailants are lured to their deaths (Matthew is hung, Andy is axed to death, while Stanley has his stomach sliced open by a speedboat propeller). The most gruesome murder is also the most appropriate: gas station attendant Johnny is invited back to Jennifer's home with promises of a more romantic liaison, but while they share a bath together Jennifer castrates him with a razor in a scene which is far less explicit than the gruesome castrations in Nagisa Ôshima's *In the Realm of the Senses* (*Ai no Corrida*, 1976) and the complete hardcore version of Derek Ford's *Sex Express* (*Diversions*, 1975) but is certainly more intense (the blood which suddenly bubbles to the surface of the bath water is unforgettable). The equivalent scene in the inevitable 2010 remake, directed by Steven R. Monroe and starring Sarah Butler, has more in common with the cycle of 'torture porn' exercises in extreme violence and mutilation as exemplified by Eli Roth's *Hostel* (2005) and *Hostel Part II* (2007), the latter featuring a resourceful Final Girl (Lauren German) who proves to be equally adept at torture and murder herself. Monroe's *I Spit on Your Grave 2* (2013) and R.D. Braunstein's *I Spit on Your Grave III: Vengeance Is Mine* (2015) continue in similar vein, while Zarchi's *I Spit on Your Grave: Deja Vu* (2018) is a formal sequel with Keaton returning as the same character.

Final Girls also populate such films as John Carpenter's *The Fog*, with Adrienne Barbeau fighting off the ghosts of dead seamen in a lighthouse which doubles as a radio station; Wes Craven's *A Nightmare on Elm Street*, whose Nancy Thompson (Heather Langenkamp) sets booby traps to dispose of dream demon Freddy Krueger (Robert Englund); and most significantly from a more mainstream perspective, Ripley (Sigourney Weaver) in the first four films of the *Alien* franchise (Ridley Scott's *Alien*, 1979, James Cameron's *Aliens*, 1986, David Fincher's *Alien 3*, 1992, and Jean-Pierre Jeunet's *Alien Resurrection*, 1997). Each of these Final Girls displays a keen understanding and awareness of the dangers that surround them, often noticing how dire the situation has become well before their soon-to-be-slayed friends.

How does all this fit in with our reluctant male hero Ash Williams? It's worth looking at all of the characters of *The Evil Dead* before casting an eye over Ash himself, however, as the four other early-twenty-somethings are rather atypical of similarly defined college students in the stalk-and-slash films of the period.

- Scott, Ash's friend and boyfriend of Shelly: it's Scott who first ventures into the cellar when the trapdoor blows open during the dinner scene, whilst Ash follows with more trepidation than daring. He's also physically stronger than Ash and not afraid to resort to violence.

- Cheryl, Ash's sister: early in the film, Cheryl is clearly marked out as the 'sensitive' one, a creative soul (an artist) but also prone to an awareness of, and aversion to, the 'horrible place'. The sketch she is making of the clock suddenly turns into a crude face, her hand is barely able to control the pencil as the whispering voice outside beckons her to 'join us'. She is also the one who senses danger in the voice on the tape recorder retrieved by Ash from the cellar.

- Linda, Ash's girlfriend, and Shelly, girlfriend of Scott: compared to Scott and Cheryl, Linda and Shelly are far less interesting and rather ill-defined, vague outlines.

None of the female characters reveal any sexual proclivities. In one POV scene from outside the bedroom window Shelly starts to undress but, crucially, Sam Raimi decides to go no further, unlike the directors of the slasher film, whose females disrobe with habitual free abandon. It's after Cheryl is attacked by the vines that Ash's heroic instincts slowly begin to take effect. Cheryl insists that they leave the cabin immediately and that Ash drive her to the nearest town, which he attempts to do until confronted with the broken, twisted bridge which was their only route out of the forest.

Ash and Scott prove to be equally adept at demon-bashing; it takes the pair of them to restrain the possessed Shelly, but Scott is the one who takes the axe and gruesomely dismembers her. Scott also shows good sense in wanting to cut (literally) and run. He and Ash have just buried what is left of Shelly and now he really doesn't care what happens to Ash and Linda. Scott also quickly succumbs to the spirits in the woods and dies of his injuries.

Fig. 22 Ash cowering in the corner.

There's no doubt that Ash has the rugged good looks of a comic book hero. Bruce Campbell — like Charles Napier, another superb character actor and a personal favourite of Jonathan Demme (Citizens Band, 1977, Something Wild, 1986, The Silence of the Lambs, 1990) and Russ Meyer (Cherry, Harry and Raquel!, 1969, Beyond the Valley of the Dolls, 1970, Supervixens, 1975) — possesses the kind of face that seems chiselled from granite. Hedy Lamarr's beauty may have been the basis for Catwoman and the model for Walt Disney's Snow White, but I wonder how many comic book artists have consciously or subconsciously drawn upon Campbell for inspiration?

He looks quite the part in his tough denim shirt brandishing an axe or shotgun, but it's only when Ash is bereft of male companionship (Scott) that the parallels with the Final Girl become apparent. Like Laurie in *Halloween* Ash is pragmatic, becomes courageous, unafraid to take risks or endanger himself. With Scott dead and yet to be reanimated, he's at the mercy of his possessed girlfriend and her dancing marionette-style routine, which is almost as creepy as Cheryl's metamorphosis into a hysterically taunting demon. With no real understanding or comprehension of the horrors that are surrounding him he finally decapitates Linda. He also soon learns how to use a shotgun; in *Halloween* Laurie is quick-thinking enough to fashion a weapon from coat-hangers, and Jennifer knows exactly what to do with a razor blade or a length of rope in *I Spit on Your Grave* (Sally, in *The Texas Chainsaw Massacre*, simply doesn't have time to think of anything, let alone any weapons; survival is all that matters).

There isn't just one demon for Ash to destroy but three once Scott reveals his possessed state. Unlike the slasher film, where the Final Girl is forced to confront the madman after he has murdered her friends, in *The Evil Dead* it is the friends that Ash (the Final Guy) has to defend himself against. Amidst all the carnage (by this time he has had to horribly gouge out Scott's eyes) a bubble seems to burst within Ash's brain: it's the Book of the Dead that's to blame, so destroy the Book and the demons will follow. After a struggle during which Scott clamps his teeth into Ash's leg and Cheryl whacks him repeatedly with a poker, Ash succeeds in throwing the Book onto the fire and the meltdown begins.

As an inverted Final Girl Ash does fulfil some of the qualities inherent in Sally Hardesty and Laurie Strode: a good-natured, calm disposition, romantic yet virginal, but most importantly resourceful. He will use whatever tools come to hand and whatever thoughts enter his head in order to survive, even if it means terrible injury. In *The Texas Chainsaw Massacre*, Sally is cut, slashed, chased through woodland and twice forced to jump through high windows, and in *Halloween* Laurie herself feels the steel of Michael's knife.

Interestingly, Tony Maylam's *The Burning* (1980) features its own variation on the Final Girl/Guy concept. An early Miramax production from the now discredited Weinstein Brothers, this otherwise conventional slasher borrows its summer camp setting and Tom Savini make-up effects from *Friday the 13th* but includes a male hero, Todd (Brian Matthews), who, once the rest of the cast have been dispatched by a madman armed with a pair of shears, must contend with a 'return of the repressed' situation as the killer is revealed to be the camp caretaker who was horribly disfigured in a fire years before – a prank-gone-wrong in which the younger Todd had participated. Final Guys also appear in such disparate genre films as *Hostel* and Jack Sholder's *A Nightmare on Elm Street Part 2: Freddy's Revenge* (1985).

One of the ways in which *The Evil Dead* is unusual in its approach to the Final Girl/Guy is that it leaves the audience guessing which one of its five protagonists will survive at the film's end. In most American horror movies of this period, and the early 1980s stalk-and-slash cycle in particular, the demographics of the narrative are largely unambiguous: if you misbehave in any way you will be dealt with severely (even *Halloween* treats its characters in this fashion). Amy Jones' *The Slumber Party Massacre* (1981) chooses not one but three potential Final Girls from its attractive cast, and they are all given the opportunity to despatch the impotent, power drill-toting psycho. Sam Raimi seems to be saying, 'None of my people are bad, they do nothing wrong or illegal, so let's see which one of them, male or female, has the courage to overcome the demons.' It pays off with the transformation of Ash into the equivalent of the Final Girl, and in this way the film bucks the dominant trend of the time by thrusting forward a male survivor who had hitherto taken a cowardly back seat.

Ash is the antithesis of the rugged macho male or the 'dumb jock' of so many early 1980s horrors; the female characters are undeniably sympathetic if vacuous in these films and their survival is often welcome, but the males tend towards the stupid and the boorish – unlike Ash Williams of *The Evil Dead*, who embodies the spirit of the Final Girl without losing his masculinity, his sense of worth or his heroic pride.

Chapter 5: 'The Number One Nasty'

By May 1981 the Renaissance partners were ready to secure a distribution deal for *The Evil Dead*. The trio set out on a journey to the West Coast, their first trip to Hollywood, but they found that Sunset Boulevard wasn't paved with gold and sprinkled with stardust. They pitched the film to Avco Embassy, Charles Fries and Paramount, but without success. Recalls Rob Tapert, 'nobody wanted it... it was turned down by everybody' (Tapert in Warren 2000: 82). Discouraged, the team instead looked to distributors in New York for interest (at this point the film was still titled *Book of the Dead*), and New Line Cinema sent out some positive signals; however the prospective deal fell through when they declined to offer an advance on world rights distribution. Still without a deal, on 15th October 1981 *The Evil Dead* was nevertheless given its grand premiere in Detroit, with the gala premiere being held in the same city the following evening.

From *Book of the Dead* to *The Evil Dead* and Stephen King

Finally, Irvin Shapiro was contacted. Shapiro's influence on American film distribution is immeasurable. A former critic for the *Washington Herald*, Shapiro founded World Pictures (later Films Around the World) in 1932, a distribution company he continued to manage until 1985. In the 1940s he headed Film Classics, which specialised in the reissues of both American and foreign films, and in the 1950s was instrumental in bringing movies to television, initially by acquiring the rights to a number of MGM productions from the previous decade. He also helped to found the Cannes Film Festival, which held its first gala at the French resort in 1946. Among the many films that Shapiro brought to American audiences are Robert Wiene's *The Cabinet of Dr. Caligari* (*Das cabinett des Dr. Caligari*, 1919), Sergei Eisenstein's *Battleship Potemkin* (*Bronenosets Potyomkin*, 1925), Jean Renoir's *La grande illusion* (1937) and Jean-Luc Godard's *À bout de souffle* (*Breathless*, 1959). He also assisted in the distribution of such diverse American productions as Martin Scorsese's *Mean Streets* (1973), Ulli Lommel's *Cocaine Cowboys* (1979) and Paul Bartel's *Eating Raoul* (1982). He's thanked in the credits of Romero's *Dawn of the Dead*, *Creepshow* (1982) and *Day of the Dead* (1985). Shapiro offered to distribute Sam Raimi's debut feature with help from New Line.

Formed in 1967 by Robert Shaye as a distribution unit specialising in foreign films – Walerian Borowczyk's *Immoral Tales* (*Contes immoraux*, 1973) and Bertrand Blier's *Get Out Your Handkerchiefs* (*Préparez vos mouchoirs*, 1976) were just two of the many films they released in the States – New Line was starting to move towards film production with Mark L. Lester's *Stunts* (1977) and John Waters' *Polyester* (1981). In 1984 they both produced and distributed *A Nightmare on Elm Street*, an extraordinary commercial success for the company, earning $25 million on a budget of $1.8 million. Through Irvin Shapiro the Renaissance team secured the international distribution rights to the film, with New Line handling US and Canadian theatrical releasing (video and television rights would be shared by the two outfits).

Shapiro's help didn't come without a few caveats, however. He was unhappy with the working title *Book of the Dead* and suggested something catchier. His original suggestion was *The Evil Dead Men and the Evil Dead Women* (Shapiro had a passion for horror movies but this title was simply too heavy-handed). *These Bitches Are Witches* was another, rather coarse, suggestion. Finally, a new title was agreed upon: the film would now be called *The Evil Dead*. Also, there were no production stills which Shapiro could use to promote the film, save for a handful of behind-the-scenes shots from on location in Tennessee. As many images as possible were taken from the negative to compensate for this shortcoming, but Shapiro still insisted on new publicity photos. One of these became the basis for the film's US theatrical poster: the eerie, somewhat brutal image of a woman whose throat is clutched by a hairy male hand while buried up to her chest in the forest soil. It's an unforgettable shot, despite there being no comparable scene in the entire film. The actress in the photo is Bridget Hoffman, who would work with Raimi, in front of and behind the camera, on *Crimewave* (1985), *Darkman* (1990) and *Army of Darkness*.

Irvin Shapiro encouraged the Renaissance partners to publicise the film in Europe with the intention of garnering as much international interest as possible, and it worked wonderfully well. *The Evil Dead* was screened out-of-competition at the 1982 Cannes Film Festival when Renaissance were touring the movie around Europe. Remembers Stephen King:

> I saw it by chance at the Cannes Film Festival when Richard Rubinstein and I were

there on a junket to publicise *Creepshow*. And it blew me away. Totally. Blew me right through the back doors, through the lobby and into the street, figuratively speaking. I was registering with like one peripheral corner of my mind that there was a lot of shit going on in the picture that was so amateurish that you could hardly believe that you were seeing it on the big screen. There was a matte of the full moon that looked like a postage stamp on a letter, if you imagine the screen as an envelope. But at the same time, even that they would try to put those shots in there with what they had was amazing. Then the larger part of my mind was registering things that I had never seen before in a movie, ever, that were working perfectly. These shots that were like insane Steadicam shots that were going on. It wouldn't stop. It was over the top, it was like a thunderstorm in a bottle, just relentless. (King in Warren 2000: 89/90)

Back in the US King wrote a glowing review of the as-yet unreleased film which appeared in the November 1982 issue of *Twilight Zone* magazine. Here are some choice extracts:

When I met Sam Raimi at the Cannes Film Festival in May 1982, my first thought was that this fellow was one of three things: a busboy, a runaway American high school student, or a genius. He wasn't a busboy, and Raimi finished high school some time ago, although he has the sort of ageless sophomore looks that are going to keep bartenders asking to see his driver's license or state liquor card until he's at least thirty-five. That he is a genius is as yet unproven; that he has made the most ferociously original horror film of 1982 seems to me beyond doubt. *The Evil Dead* has the simple, stupid power of a good campfire story – but its simplicity is not a side effect. It is something carefully crafted by Raimi, who is anything but stupid. In *Evil Dead* the camera has the kind of nightmarish fluidity that we associate with the early John Carpenter; it dips and slides and then zooms in so fast you want to plaster your hands over your eyes. What Raimi achieves in *Evil Dead* is a black rainbow of horror. (King 1982: 20-21)

PALACE PICTURES AND THE SCALA CINEMA

Born in London in 1956, Stephen Woolley had worked as an usher at the Screen on the Green cinema in Islington before becoming the manager of The Other Cinema in 1976, a radical film collective 'aligned with a worldwide political avant-garde, revolutionary and innovative, a counter-cultural playground for experimentation and adventurous programming' (Giles 2018: 11). Formed in 1969 by Leslie Elliot, Nick Hart-Williams and Peter Sainsbury, The Other Cinema was based at a number of different venues, including the King's Cross Cinema, before settling at the 400-seat basement auditorium of the Scala Theatre in Fitzrovia in 1974. As front-of-house manager, Woolley quickly began to twist The Other Cinema's programming in an unexpected direction while continuing to honour the collective's commitment towards politically and socially aware features and documentaries. In July and August of 1977, a four-week season of movies (Frank Tashlin's *The Girl Can't Help It* (1956), Richard Thorpe's *Jailhouse Rock* (1957), Bob Rafelson's *Head* (1968), Jean-Luc Godard's *One Plus One* (*Sympathy for the Devil*, 1969)) and live performances (Aswad, Shakin' Stevens and the Sunsets, Squeeze, the Tom Robinson Band) proved enormously successful. However, mounting financial difficulties (principally funding concerns, as the British Film Institute's interest in The Other Cinema, which by this time had ceased to be a collective, had all but evaporated) led to its closure in January 1978.

It was Nick Hart-Williams who decided to resurrect The Other Cinema as the Scala in May of that year, with Stephen Woolley as manager. The Scala's early years were a mixture of the type of programming previously associated with The Other Cinema combined with Woolley's passion for Hollywood's Golden Age (Joshua Logan's *Bus Stop*, 1956, Samuel Fuller's *Forty Guns*, 1957), world cinema (Akira Kurosawa's *Seven Samurai / Shichinin no Samurai*, 1954, Pier Paolo Pasolini's *Salò, or the 120 Days of Sodom / Salò o le 120 giornate di Sodoma*, 1975), underground cinema (Jean Genet's *Un chant d'amour*, 1950, Curt McDowell's *Thundercrack!*, 1975), horror (Tod Browning's *Freaks*, 1932, David Lynch's *Eraserhead*, 1976), music (Perry Henzell's *The Harder They Come*, 1972, Julien Temple's *The Great Rock 'n' Roll Swindle*, 1979), science fiction (Nathan Juran's *Attack of the 50ft. Woman*, 1958, Edward Bernds' *Queen of Outer Space*, 1958), exploitation (Roger Corman's *The Trip*, 1967, George Miller's *Mad Max*, 1979) and cult TV (*The Avengers*, 1961–1969, *The Prisoner*, 1967–1968).

Thanks to the astonishing breadth of Woolley's eclectic approach to programming UK audiences were introduced (and also reintroduced) to the work of Bernardo Bertolucci, Walerian Borowczyk, Luis Buñuel, Jean Cocteau, Roger Corman, David Cronenberg,

Rainer Werner Fassbinder, Federico Fellini, Samuel Fuller, Jean-Luc Godard, Werner Herzog, Alfred Hitchcock, Derek Jarman, Akira Kurosawa, Sergio Leone, Pier Paolo Pasolini, Sam Peckinpah, Roman Polanski, Jacques Rivette, Nicolas Roeg, Ken Russell, Martin Scorsese, Andrei Tarkovsky, Luchino Visconti, Peter Watkins, Orson Welles and Ed Wood. The Scala unleashed *Freaks*, *Thundercrack!*, *Eraserhead*, *In the Realm of the Senses*, John Waters' *Pink Flamingos* (1972) and Marco Ferreri's *The Last Woman / La dernière femme* (1976) on an unsuspecting and totally unprepared London public, although the Scala's audience was also drawn from all parts of the United Kingdom and encouraged renewed interest into the films of Humphrey Bogart, Marlon Brando, Louise Brooks, Joan Crawford, James Dean and Marilyn Monroe.

Double and triple-bills and weekend all-nighters became synonymous with the Scala. Blue Mondays featured Walerian Borowczyk or Russ Meyer triple-bills, *Thundercrack!* was frequently paired with Stephen Sayadian's futuristic post-punk porno *Café Flesh* (1982), while there were all-night horror, science fiction and Clint Eastwood marathons on Saturdays.

In May 1981 the Scala relocated to King's Cross (at that time an extremely rough, grubby area of North London rife with prostitution and drug-dealing) at the 478-seat Victorian picture palace which had been home to The Other Cinema for a few months a decade earlier. The Scala's new location provided the perfect backdrop to showcase the cutting-edge of cult and world cinema. The auditorium was dark, cavernous and cold, where illicit pleasures could be found at any time of the day and night (the back row became a disreputable cruising ground). For the next 11 years, the Scala continued to thrive against all the odds; independently run, it fought long and hard to survive financial hardship, but in 1993 it all began to unravel. On 1st April 1992, the Scala had programmed Lindsay Anderson's *If...* (1968) with a 'Surprise Film': Stanley Kubrick's *A Clockwork Orange* (1971). Kubrick, unhappy with the British media's perception of the film as inciting real-life violence, had withdrawn the film from UK distribution in 1973 ('the most effective banning in British film censorship', Matthews 1994: 209), which meant that even cinemas such as the Scala, which held a special licence allowing them to screen uncertificated movies, could not legally show the film. Warner Bros., the distributor, took legal action on 23rd March 1993. The Scala lost the breach-of-copyright trial and it was effectively sunk: the cinema closed its doors on 5th June that year, one month before the lease on the building at 275-277 Pentonville Road was due to expire.

Inextricably linked to the Scala during its King's Cross years was Palace Pictures, a distribution and, later, production company formed in 1982 by the Scala's Stephen Woolley and Nik Powell (1950–2019), who had been co-founder with Richard Branson of the Virgin Group. Initially Palace focused on the burgeoning home video market; among the many films distributed on video by Palace in the UK, firstly as rental titles and by the end of the decade as sell-through releases, were such staple Scala fare as *The Hills Have Eyes*, Samuel Fuller's *Shock Corridor* (1963) and *The Naked Kiss* (1964), Wim Wenders' *The American Friend / Der Amerikanische freund* (1977) and *Paris, Texas* (1984), Frank Henenlotter's *Basket Case* (1981), Rainer Werner Fassbinder's *Querelle* (1982), Dario Argento's *Phenomena / Creepers* (1985) and Werner Herzog's *Cobra Verde* (1987). In March of 1982 Woolley and Powell visited the American Film Market in Los Angeles and procured the British distribution rights to *The Evil Dead* (the first time that the film had been sold to a distributor) for £65,000. Back in Britain Woolley's approach to distribution was as wild as the films he was programming at the Scala: realising that there was a divergence in cinema and video audiences Woolley and Powell's radical strategy was to release *The Evil Dead* simultaneously on home video (VHS and Beta) and to cinemas. Employing Paul Webster as head of theatrical distribution to oversee a marketing campaign built around word-of-mouth preview screenings (the film opened in Scotland before touring the rest of the UK), the Palace duo also brought on board freelance artist Graham Humphreys to design the theatrical poster and video artwork; his vivid, garish imagery became crucial to establishing interest in the film and is instantly recognisable to this day, frequently recycled for DVD and Blu-ray promotional displays.

THE EVIL DEAD AT THE SCALA

The Scala previewed *The Evil Dead* on Friday 8th October 1982 at 11.15pm, a surprise screening as it replaced the scheduled *Basket Case*, Frank Henelotter's delightfully sleazy first feature. Recalls Scala regular Neil Irving: 'There were about six of us in the whole cinema. And it was one of the best ever experiences in the cinema. We had no idea what to expect – the film scared and exhilarated us – we were cowering in our seats. And the Scala cat kept jumping on us throughout which added to the tension' (Irving in Giles 2018: 138). The film was previewed again, officially this time, on New Year's Day 1983 as part of a quartet of horror movie previews, an experiment which was so successful that it would continue annually until January 1992. Starting at 5pm, when most audiences' hangovers might have worn off, the other films being screened were *Basket Case*, Bruno Mattei's *Zombie Creeping Flesh / Inferno dei morti-viventi* (1980) and Eric Weston's *Evilspeak* (1981). *The Evil Dead* was programmed 33 times between 1982 and 1992; it played double and triple-bills and all-nighters alongside other Scala favourites like *Night of the Living Dead*, *The Hills Have Eyes*, *Dawn of the Dead*, *Zombie Flesh Eaters*, *Blood Simple*, *A Nightmare on Elm Street*, *Crimewave*, *Day of the Dead*, *Phenomena* and *Evil Dead II*.[1]

Graham Humphreys' now-iconic poster art was the perfect accompaniment to the marketing campaign devised by Woolley, Powell and Webster. In her magnificent history of the Scala Cinema, Jane Giles describes the artwork as 'splenetic, acid-trip colours and zombie faces... the artist's *Citizen Kane*, hitting the zeitgeist and forever after referred to as one of Humphreys' defining works' (Giles 2018: 154). And, crucially, the Scala audience also contributed to making the film into a roaring box-office success. Try and imagine what it must have been like viewing *The Evil Dead* in the early hours of a Sunday morning at the Scala during one of its many all-night screenings ('All-Night Evil Nightmares'), none too sure of who might be sitting next to you in the dark auditorium, while a beam of blue light from the projection booth pierces the blackness, capturing the dust and smoke as its glow passes over you and projecting onto the screen a gruesome, eye-popping classic of horror cinema.

THE 'VIDEO NASTIES'

The term 'nasty', to identify a work of disreputable, often violent or horrific nature, was first used in the literary press to describe the early novels of British horror author James Herbert, in particular *The Rats* (1974), about an infestation of giant rats in London's East End, and *The Fog* (1975), in which a lethal mist is released from beneath the earth and turns the population into psychopaths. Mary Whitehouse popularised the phrase 'video nasty' in 1982 but it is likely that the *Sunday People* newspaper was the first to use it in a December 1981 article on the deeply suspect content of many of the films which were appearing on the shelves of video shops across the country for private viewing in the home. In the early 1980s the home video market was wild, unruly and, most importantly, unregulated. Fly-by-night distributors released anything and everything they could get their hands on for a fair price, and the quality of the prints their acquisitions were struck from was of little importance. The British Board of Film Censors (BBFC) – 'Classification' would replace 'Censors' in 1984 – was responsible for ensuring that cinema releases were awarded a specific rating, or certificate, based on a code of practice that involved film censorship and minimum age restrictions: sex and violence were top of the BBFC's agenda when classifying a film for theatrical release, political censorship less so. However, due to a lack of awareness of how film viewing habits were beginning to change with the increasing popularity of the VCR, films released on to video were not required to be submitted to the BBFC for approval. This meant that a whole galaxy of weird, subversive and, frequently, *outré* works were widely available for the first time to the British public to rent or to purchase. Some of the films – including Golden Age porno such as Joe Sherman's *Ms. Magnificent* (1977) and Anthony Spinelli's *Vista Valley PTA* (1980) – would doubtless have been heavily censored or banned outright were they submitted to the Board for classification, and a fair number of titles which found their way into video stores had already given the BBFC a headache when they were up for cinema release – *The Exorcist* (1973), *The Texas Chainsaw Massacre*, Sam Peckinpah's *Straw Dogs* (1971), Wes Craven's *The Last House on the Left* (1972) and Tinto Brass' *Caligula* (1979) to name a few.

Due to the overall lack of any regulation by the BBFC, the subject of home video soon fell under the remit of the Obscene Publications Act, 1959. How could the OPA be used to regulate video? It simply couldn't, but it could be used as a means of prosecuting any video which the Director of Public Prosecutions (DPP) deemed 'obscene' and a violation of the law. Spurred on by a shockingly misinformed 'moral panic' led by Mary Whitehouse (a socially conservative campaigner against 'filth' in the British media and society as a whole) and the tabloid press, whose headlines and articles ('Rape of Our Children's Minds', *Daily Mail*, 30th June 1983) reeked of ignorance and confirmed a very real contempt for the subject matter and the films under discussion, the Video Recordings Act (VRA) was pushed through by a puzzled Parliament. Becoming law on 1st September 1985, this enabled the banning of any film considered to be a 'video nasty'. Martin Barker identifies the popular press construction of the 'nasty' as follows: 'Bad acting, bad filming, no real storyline; endless successions of scenes of sex and violence, with no real reason for showing them; everything cheap and poorly done' (Barker 1984: 105). More formally, under the terms of the VRA, the BBFC was required to classify all video titles (with the notable exception of some sport and music related videos); any film not submitted to the Board for approval could not be hired or sold and would therefore be effectively illegal. The VRA had its origins in a Private Members' Bill put to the House of Commons by Graham Bright, Conservative MP for Luton South, who described the 'nasties' as 'grossly offensive to all reasonable people' (Bright in Barker 1984: 23). Key to the Act becoming law was the supposed effect of the viewing of a 'video nasty' on children's mental health. From the *Daily Mirror*, 25th November 1983: 'Violent, sadistic and perverted video films are as great a danger to a child's mind as any infectious disease is to the body. Yet children are being exposed to them every day. High street retailers, so obsessed with profit that they have these films on their shelves, plumb the depths of greed... these obscenities can be bought or hired in any town' (quoted in Barker 1984: 57). Martin Barker declared that the Bill 'by its own definitions and operations, gives frighteningly extensive powers to a Home Secretary [at the time, Leon Brittan] who becomes, in effect, a simple state censor – but all cloaked under the respectability of a bill designed to "protect children"' (Barker 1984: 18). Astonishingly, in 2009 the VRA was itself deemed illegal as the European Commission had not been given prior notice of its implementation; the government then responded by initiating the Video Recordings Act 2010, effectively the same legislation but with amendments to include the Digital Economy Act 2010. Unfortunately, what could not be repealed or challenged were any successful prosecutions against retailers or distributors.

THE 'VIDEO NASTY' LIST ('THE BIG 72')

The DPP began to draw up a list of 'video nasties' in the spring of 1983. 'Nasties are far removed from traditional suspense and horror films. They dwell on gory scenes of murder, rape, sado-masochism, cannibalism and Nazi atrocities' (*Sunday Times*, 23rd May 1982). The list perfectly captures this statement, although it changed frequently, with some titles being added while others were removed permanently. But one factor remained constant: a total of 72 films were considered liable for prosecution under the OPA and of this number 39 were successfully charged. In a frightening echo of the Nazi book-burnings in Berlin in 1933, copies were sometimes destroyed following seizure. Consider this article in the *Daily Mail*, 1st September 1982, titled 'Video "Nasties" to Be Destroyed':

> Two video films featuring bloody scenes of torture, mutilation and murder were ordered to be destroyed yesterday.
>
> Magistrates made the order in the first case brought by the Director of Public Prosecutions against ultra-explicit horror videos, now widely available throughout Britain.
>
> Yesterday's case was heard in Willesden, London, N., because that was where almost 600 cassettes of the two American-made videos – *Driller Killer* and *Death Trap* – were seized from British distributors, Vipco, in June.
>
> The three Willesden magistrates took only 20 minutes to agree to the DPP's application for forfeiture of *Driller Killer* and *Death Trap*, without seeing either film. They made their decision on seeing the lurid covers and after hearing Mr. Stephen Wooler, prosecuting for the DPP, describe the slaughter they depicted. *Driller Killer*, he told the court, could 'only be described as violence of most sickening nature'.
>
> *Death Trap*, he said, was an uncut version of an X-certificate cinema film of the same name. 'It is a very sick production indeed,' Mr. Wooler said.
>
> Mr. Alex Cranbrook, for Vipco, said the company agreed that the two videos were legally obscene and had co-operated fully with the DPP and the Obscene Publications Branch of Scotland Yard.

The above statement regarding the magistrates' conviction of the films purely on the basis of their cover art is particularly telling; it betrays not only a complete misunderstanding of the works on trial but also a fear that the content concealed within is too shocking, unbearable and, perhaps, too 'corruptible' to be viewed by any member of the British public, even by learned dignitaries of the judicial system (the cover of *The Driller Killer* (1979) depicts the only truly gory sequence in the film, most of the other killings taking place in semi-darkness). Interestingly, 1970s editions of Herbert Van Thal's

Pan Books of Horror Stories featured especially lurid covers (severed heads in buckets, rats crawling over human skulls) and Guy N. Smith's revolt-of-nature paperbacks (*Night of the Crabs*, 1976, *Killer Crabs*, 1978, *The Origin of the Crabs*, 1979, *Crabs on the Rampage*, 1981) were gruesomely illustrated and prefigured the approach by video companies to marketing their titles with an emphasis on their blood-soaked 'nastiness'.

Fig. 23 Abel Ferrara's The Driller Killer.

Fig. 24 Ruggero Deodato's Cannibal Holocaust.

The *Mail* continued to raise public awareness of the 'nasties' again on 23rd February 1983 ('Fine for Video "Nasties" Trader'):

Film library owner Stephen Taylor yesterday became the first person to be fined for hiring out video 'nasties'. Police who raided his shop in Leeds took away 61 tapes, including four horror videos – *Driller Killer*, *SS Experiment Camp*, *I Spit on Your Grave* and *Cannibal Holocaust*. Fining him £600 and ordering all the films to be forfeited, Stipendiary Magistrate David Loy warned Taylor and other dealers that they could face jail for selling such tapes. He said: 'Trading in this sort of filth will not be tolerated.' Mr. Robert Drybrough-Smith, prosecuting for the DPP, said it was the first time a horror video had been dealt with under Section 2 of the [Obscene Publications] Act.

A complete list of the 'Big 72' (as they became known to horror fans) can be found in the endnotes which follow this chapter.[2]

'THAT EVIL FILM'

In his otherwise excellent and long out-of-print study, *The Video Nasties*, published in 1984 while the debate over 'obscene' videos was still raging and at its most hysterical, Martin Barker singles out 10 of the films on the DPP's list for special consideration: *Cannibal ferox*, *Cannibal Holocaust*, *Don't Go in the House*, *Don't Go Near the Park*, *The Driller Killer*, *Eaten Alive / Death Trap*, *Faces of Death*, *I Spit on Your Grave*, *The Last House on the Left* and *SS Experiment Camp*. In Barker's view, these films are '...simply disgusting exercises in sadism, films put together as excuses for portraying – vividly and terrifyingly – all the things most likely to disturb and degrade, and arouse in their viewers the very worst potentialities. They are exploitation films, using all that is perverse and perverting purely for the sake of money' (Barker 1984: 104). Barker's assertions are wholly inaccurate in this respect and contextually inconclusive (admittedly, the main thrust of his book is an examination of the role of the British media in perpetuating a myth surrounding the proliferation of 'violent' and 'obscene' videos which lead directly to state censorship of the video industry) and, arguably, four of the films he discusses in his chapter 'Nasties: A Problem of Identification' (*Cannibal Holocaust*, *The Driller Killer*, *Eaten Alive*, *The Last House on the Left*) are immensely powerful works which have been considerably re-evaluated and re-appraised over the last 25 years.

So how and why did *The Evil Dead* get caught up in the hysteria surrounding 'video nasties'? How could a film which delights in taking demonic possession and bodily dismemberment to such an absurd level ever be taken so seriously by the moral guardians of British society? The answer could be that it is unapologetically over-the-top and *doesn't* take itself seriously. It never once pretends to aspire to great art, which was never the intention of the Renaissance team. They simply wanted to make a horror movie that was fun, scary, a wild carnival ghost train ride where the engine refuses to stop and just keeps on going. 'Any cinematic distinction between fast-moving, innovative examples of the horror genre like *The Evil Dead* and the static dismemberment of women or animals which distinguished other "nasties" was lost' (Matthews 1994: 240), with Mary Whitehouse famously labelling *The Evil Dead* 'the number one nasty' (Whitehouse in Matthews 1994: 242) and 'that evil film' (Whitehouse in Martin 1993: 71). It was vital to the success of *The Evil Dead* in Britain that Palace Pictures found themselves in the unique position to market the film so effectively, and it is a testament to their skill and perseverance that *The Evil Dead*'s reputation was solidly grounded. Contemporary British reviews of the film tended to reflect the deeply felt ambivalence towards horror on the one hand, and undisguised loathing on the other. Here's an extract from Clive James' review in the *Observer*, 23rd December 1984:

> When the zombie erupts from the prop-leaf mold and comes lurching through the dry-ice fumes... we decline to be alarmed because we are too busy wondering why the silly cow agreed to stay the night, the surrounding territory being so obviously crammed with recumbent zombies. She stayed in order to be haunted. She has no motivation, only a function, which is to get torn apart. The screenplay is all effects and no story. In other words, the people who made the movie care about nothing except movies.

Thankfully, not all critics shared James' sneering superiority. The always perceptive Kim Newman in the *Monthly Film Bulletin*, November 1982, declared that 'the screeching possessees here recall Dario Argento, and their messy, startling fates evoke the dread Lucio Fulci, *The Evil Dead* is more successful than its Italian precursors' (Newman 1982: 264). In the January 1983 issue of *Starburst*, Phil Edwards recognised the level of imagination and cinematic technique on display: 'Raimi never goes for the easy scare, and though there are plenty of shocks emerging from all parts of the frame, they are rarely the obvious' (Edwards 1983: 10).

Here's a typically unpretentious review of the film from the London listings publication *Time Out*:

> Raimi's first feature, a sensationally bad taste effort which narrates the rapid decline into demonic mental and physical possession of a clean-cut, all-American holiday party holed up in a mountain Tennessee retreat. The woods come alive, devils possess the living, and Tom Sullivan's amazing make-up effects climax with a final fiery exorcism which makes George Romero look like *Playschool*. Short on characterisation and plot but strong on atmospheric horror and visual churns, this movie blends comic fantasy (EC Tales) with recent genre gems like *Carrie* and *Texas Chainsaw Massacre* to impressive effect. (n.d.)

THE BRITISH CENSORSHIP OF *THE EVIL DEAD*

> At the film's actual examination in front of the Board [then BBFC Director James] Ferman and one of the examiners soon gave way to howls of laughter at 'the enormous gunk coming out of the walls and the blood spewing everywhere in all different colours'. The other examiner present, however (Ferman refused to identify either of them), remained ominously silent and once the film was over she vented her feelings. She was 'nauseated', it had 'affected her physically'; in fact her 'bodily integrity had been attacked'. Ferman decided that, if the film was going to have that sort of effect on some people he had better 'take it down a little bit'. (Matthews 1994: 242)

The Evil Dead was passed with an 'X' certificate for cinema exhibition in 1982 with 49 seconds of cuts to a number of key scenes to reduce the level of gore and violence; these included the pencil being repeatedly twisted into Linda's ankle, demon Shelly gnawing away at her hand, Scott's dismemberment of Shelly, the battering of demon Linda's head by Ash, the spurting of blood from Linda's neck after she is decapitated, and the gouging of demon Scott's eyes. The Palace video release was identical to the BBFC-authorised cinema version, yet this didn't prevent the film from being targeted by the DPP, who soon added the title to their list of videos which were potentially 'harmful' and 'obscene' under the OPA. *The Evil Dead* was first seized by police in Manchester but the copies were subsequently returned once the authorities realised that the film was actually the approved cinema version. But the seizures continued, along with bewilderment from video retailers that what the BBFC had passed for exhibition in UK cinemas was somehow illegal on video.

The following article appeared in the *Sunday Times* on 13th May 1984 under the headline 'Home Video on Trial':

> Can a film that has been given a certificate by the British Board of Film Censors deprave and corrupt? This is the question that a jury will have to consider at Leeds Crown Court next week when Barkers Videotape Centres appear on May 16 charged under Section 2 of the Obscene Publications Act.
>
> The case follows a series of raids on video retailers in recent months by the police. The Leeds case is the first time that two films with cinema certificates – *The Evil Dead*, distributed by Palace Video, and *The Burning*, from Thorn-EMI, will have been tried in front of a jury.
>
> Palace, who have decided to support Barkers together with Thorn-EMI, are expected to call a number of expert witnesses to testify as to what they consider to be the artistic quality of the films. Palace also plans to point to their track record of supporting unknown filmmakers including Sam Raimi who directed *Evil Dead*.
>
> 'At the moment the legal situation is very confused,' said Irvine Rappaport of Palace Video. 'I've asked the police how we are supposed to know if a video is obscene even if it has a certificate and they said that I should ask our solicitors. But when I asked if they had any more chance of knowing than I did they said probably not.'
>
> At the moment there seems no clear guidelines as to what is obscene. It is believed that the police have indicated unofficially that they want to retain the power to prosecute videos. But provided that the Board does not adopt what they consider to be a too liberal attitude they have said that in practice they will rarely prosecute.

As John Martin explains further in his book *The Seduction of the Gullible*:

> In an attempt to clarify the position in a test case, Palace subsidised the defence costs of the Leeds-based Barker Video Group, three branches of which had been raided in April 1983. The cloak and dagger police operation that had resulted in this bust adds

several further bizarre twists to the story: a constable had joined the club, giving a bogus address, to gather evidence, although Barker already had 75 members of the West Yorkshire Police on their membership rolls, one of their shops was managed by the wife of a Detective Sergeant, and they had invited police to vet their stock when they opened! Palace backed Barker to the hilt, even flying Raimi over to testify at the trial... in May 1984, *The Evil Dead* was unanimously acquitted.

Emboldened by the outcome of the Leeds case, dealers began to contest the 'obscenity' of *The Evil Dead* in the Crown Courts. On 1st December 1984... at Lewes Crown Court, Tony Bingham, the proprietor of Peacehaven's 'That's Entertainment', was found guilty and fined £50 each for stocking *Bloody Moon*, *Night of the Demon* and *Pretty Peaches*, but acquitted over *The Evil Dead* (the jury failing to reach a clear-cut verdict on Lucio Fulci's *Zombie Flesh Eaters*). 'Out of all the films,' the judge had commented in his summing up, '[*The Evil Dead*] dealt within the realm of fantasy much more than any of the others, and perhaps the jury should think of it in a different light.' (Martin 1993: 73)

Nik Powell was himself charged in September 1984 at Waltham Forest Magistrate's Court of possessing and distributing 'obscenity' (all copies of *The Evil Dead* were literally spirited out of the Scala in case the police raided the Palace Video offices located above the cinema). Predictably, he was acquitted at Snaresbrook Crown Court in July 1985, with the presiding judge unusually awarding Powell's costs against the DPP. In September 1985, *The Evil Dead* was finally removed from the list of banned 'video nasties' following the introduction of the VRA.

In 1987 Palace proposed submitting *The Evil Dead* to the BBFC for video certification, but James Ferman felt that it was still too soon after the 'nasty' panic, and besides he wanted to make more cuts to the film if it was to receive an '18' certificate (the ratings system had changed in November 1982, with the adults-only 'X' being replaced with the '18', although the definition remained the same for both theatrical and video releases). Nik Powell and Stephen Woolley declined to accept further censorship at this time, but in March 1990 *The Evil Dead* finally received its long-overdue video classification. In addition to the 49 seconds of cuts previously made in 1982 the Board insisted on an additional one minute 55 seconds of cuts. The extra trims included extensive cutting to the tree rape; more cuts to the scratching, biting and chewing of hands and legs; and headless demon Linda spraying blood over Ash. Since 2000, however, all subsequent releases of *The Evil Dead* on DVD and Blu-ray have been passed uncut by the BBFC.

Notes

1. Other films which were regularly screened alongside *The Evil Dead* at the Scala included Herschell Gordon Lewis' *Color Me Blood Red* (1964), Ted V. Mikels' *The Corpse Grinders* (1971), Vicente Aranda's *The Blood Spattered Bride / La novia ensangrentada* (1972), William Friedkin's *The Exorcist* (1973), Paul Morrissey's *Flesh for Frankenstein / Il mostro è in tavola... Barone Frankenstein* (1973), Antony Balch's *Horror Hospital* (1973), Larry Cohen's *It's Alive* (1973), Jorge Grau's *The Living Dead at the Manchester Morgue / No profanar el sueno de los muertos* (1974), Tobe Hooper's *Eaten Alive / Death Trap* (1976) and *The Funhouse* (1981), Jeff Lieberman's *Squirm* (1976) and *Just Before Dawn* (1980), Mario Bava's *Shock* (1977), Abel Ferrara's *The Driller Killer* (1979), Ulli Lommel's *The Boogey Man / The Bogey Man* (1980), Lucio Fulci's *City of the Living Dead / Paura nella città dei morti viventi* (1980), *The Beyond / ...E tu vivrai nel terrore! L'Aldila* (1981) and *The House By the Cemetery / Quella villa accanto al cimitero* (1981), Dario Argento's *Tenebrae* (1982), John Carpenter's *The Thing* (1982), David Cronenberg's *Shivers / The Parasite Murders* (1974) and *Videodrome* (1982), Dan O'Bannon's *The Return of the Living Dead* (1984), Stuart Gordon's *Re-Animator* (1985) and *From Beyond* (1986), Frank Henenlotter's *Brain Damage* (1987), Clive Barker's *Hellraiser* (1987) and Richard Stanley's *Hardware* (1990).

2. Listed alphabetically under the title they were released in the UK, this is the 'Big 72' (* successfully prosecuted by the DPP):
   - *Absurd / Rosso sangue* (Joe D'Amato, 1981)*
   - *Anthropophagus* (Joe D'Amato, 1980)*
   - *The Axe* (Frederick R. Friedel, 1977)*
   - *Bay of Blood / Ecologia del delitto* (Mario Bava, 1971)*
   - *The Beast in Heat / La bestia in calore* (Luigi Batzella, 1977)*
   - *The Beyond / ...E tu vivrai nel terrore! L'Aldila* (Lucio Fulci, 1981)
   - *Blood Feast* (Herschell Gordon Lewis, 1963)*
   - *Blood Rites / The Ghastly Ones* (Andy Milligan, 1968)*
   - *Bloody Moon / Die säge des todes* (Jess Franco, 1980)*
   - *The Bogey Man / The Boogeyman* (Ulli Lommel, 1980)
   - *The Burning* (Tony Maylam, 1980)*
   - *Cannibal Apocalypse / Apocalisse domani* (Antonio Margheriti, 1980)*

- *Cannibal ferox* (Umberto Lenzi, 1981)*
- *Cannibal Holocaust* (Ruggero Deodato, 1979)*
- *The Cannibal Man / La semana del asesino / The Apartment on the 13th Floor* (Eloy de la Iglesia, 1972)*
- *Cannibal Terror / Terreur cannibale* (Alain Deruelle / Olivier Mathot / Julio Pérez Tabernero, 1980)
- *Contamination* (Luigi Cozzi, 1980)
- *Dead and Buried* (Gary Sherman, 1981)
- *Death Trap / Eaten Alive* (Tobe Hooper, 1976)
- *Deep River Savages / Il paese del sesso selvaggio* (Umberto Lenzi, 1972)
- *Delirium* (Peter Maris, 1979)
- *The Devil Hunter / El caníbal* (Jess Franco, 1980)*
- *Don't Go in the House* (Joseph Ellison, 1980)
- *Don't Go in the Woods* (James Bryan, 1980)*
- *Don't Go Near the Park* (Lawrence D. Foldes, 1979)
- *Don't Look in the Basement / The Forgotten* (S.F. Brownrigg, 1973)
- *The Driller Killer* (Abel Ferrara, 1979)*
- *The Evil Dead* (Sam Raimi, 1981)
- *Evilspeak* (Eric Weston, 1981)*
- *Exposé* (James Kenelm Clarke, 1975)*
- *Faces of Death* (Conan LeClaire, 1978)*
- *Fight for Your Life* (Robert A. Endelson, 1977)*
- *Flesh for Frankenstein / Il mostro è in tavola... Barone Frankenstein)* (Paul Morrissey, 1973)*
- *Forest of Fear / Bloodeaters* (Chuck McCrann, 1979)*
- *Frozen Scream* (Frank Roach, 1975)
- *The Funhouse* (Tobe Hooper, 1981)
- *The Gestapo's Last Orgy / L'Ultima orgia del III Reich* (Cesare Canevari, 1976)*
- *The House By the Cemetery / Quella villa accanto al cimitero* (Lucio Fulci, 1981)*
- *The House on the Edge of the Park / La casa sperduta nel parco* (Ruggero Deodato, 1980)*
- *Human Experiments* (J. Gregory Goodell, 1979)
- *I Miss You, Hugs and Kisses* (Murray Markowitz, 1978)
- *Inferno* (Dario Argento, 1980)
- *Island of Death / Ta pedhia tou dhiavolou* (Nico Mastorakis, 1975)*
- *I Spit on Your Grave* (Meir Zarchi, 1978)*
- *The Killer Nun / Suor omicidi* (Giulio Berruti, 1978)
- *The Last House on the Left* (Wes Craven, 1972)*
- *Late Night Trains / L'Ultimo treno della notte / Night Train Murders* (Aldo Lado, 1974)
- *The Living Dead at the Manchester Morgue / No profanar el sueno de los muertos* (Jorge Grau,

1974)
- *Love Camp 7* (Lee Frost, 1969)*
- *Madhouse* (Ovidio G. Assonitis, 1981)*
- *Mardi Gras Massacre* (Jack Weis, 1978)*
- *Nightmare Maker / Butcher, Baker, Nightmare Maker* (William Asher, 1981)
- *Nightmares in a Damaged Brain / Nightmare* (Romano Scavolini, 1981)*
- *Night of the Bloody Apes / La Horriplante Bestia Humana* (René Cardona, 1968)*
- *Night of the Demon* (James C. Wasson, 1980)*
- *Possession* (Andrzej Zulawski, 1981)
- *Pranks / The Dorm That Dripped Blood* (Stephen Carpenter / Jeffrey Obrow, 1981)
- *Prisoner of the Cannibal God / La montagna del dio cannibale / Mountain of the Cannibal God* (Sergio Martino, 1978)
- *Revenge of the Bogey Man / Boogeyman II* (Bruce Starr, 1982)
- *The Slayer* (J.S. Cardone, 1982)
- *Snuff* (Michael Findlay, 1974)*
- *SS Experiment Camp / Lager SSadis kastrat kommandantur* (Sergio Garrone, 1976)*
- *Tenebrae* (Dario Argento, 1982)*
- *Terror Eyes / Night School* (Ken Hughes, 1980)
- *The Toolbox Murders* (Dennis Donnelly, 1977)
- *Unhinged* (Don Gronquist, 1982)
- *Visiting Hours* (Jean-Claude Lord, 1981)
- *The Werewolf and the Yeti / La maldicion de la bestia / Night of the Howling Beast* (Miguel Iglesias Bonns, 1975)*
- *The Witch Who Came from the Sea* (Matteo Ottaviano, 1976)
- *Women Behind Bars / Das diamants pour l'enfer* (Jess Franco, 1975)
- *Zombie Creeping Flesh / Inferno dei morti-viventi* (Bruno Mattei, 1980)
- *Zombie Flesh Eaters / Zombi 2* (Lucio Fulci, 1979)*

In addition, the DPP compiled a further list of titles, 82 films in total which could not be prosecuted in the same way as the 'Big 72', but were still considered potentially 'obscene' and liable for seizure. Again, like the primary list, the films under consideration differed wildly in quality, subject matter and conception. The titles which the less-than-cine-literate police and prosecutors were instructed to watch out for included the following:
- *The Blue Eyes of the Broken Doll / Los ojos azules de la muñeca rota* (Carlos Aured, 1973)
- *Cannibal / Ultimo mondo cannibale / The Last Cannibal World* (Ruggero Deodato, 1976)
- *The Cannibals / Mondo cannibale* (Jess Franco, 1980)
- *Deep Red / Profondo rosso* (Dario Argento, 1975)
- *The Demons / Les démons* (Jess Franco, 1972)

- *Eaten Alive / Mangiati vivi* (Umberto Lenzi, 1980)
- *The Erotic Rites of Frankenstein / La maldicion de Frankenstein* (Jess Franco, 1972)
- *Foxy Brown* (Jack Hill, 1974)
- *The Hills Have Eyes* (Wes Craven, 1977)
- *Inseminoid* (Norman J. Warren, 1980)
- *The Last Hunter / L'Ultimo cacciatore* (Antonio Margheriti, 1980)
- *Mark of the Devil / Hexen bis aufs blut gequaelt* (Michael Armstrong, 1969)
- *Martin* (George Romero, 1976)
- *Nightmare City / Incubo sulla città contaminata* (Umberto Lenzi, 1980)
- *Night of the Living Dead* (George Romero, 1968)
- *Oasis of the Zombies / La tumba de los muertos vivientes* (Jess Franco, 1981)
- *Phantasm* (Don Coscarelli, 1977)
- *Prey* (Norman J. Warren, 1977)
- *Rabid* (David Cronenberg, 1976)
- *Scanners* (David Cronenberg, 1980)
- *Suspiria* (Dario Argento, 1976)
- *Terror* (Norman J. Warren, 1978)
- *The Texas Chainsaw Massacre* (Tobe Hooper, 1974)
- *The Thing* (John Carpenter, 1982)
- *Tomb of the Living Dead / The Mad Doctor of Blood Island* (Gerardo DeLeon / Eddie Romero, 1969)
- *Zombie Holocaust / La regina dei cannibali* (Marino Girolami, 1979)
- *Zombie Lake / El lago de los muertos vivients / Zombies' Lake* (Jean Rollin, 1980)
- *Zombies: Dawn of the Dead / Dawn of the Dead* (George Romero, 1978)

CHAPTER 6: THE INFLUENCE AND LEGACY OF *THE EVIL DEAD*

Sam Raimi's 1985 follow-up to *The Evil Dead* was *Crimewave*, co-written by Joel and Ethan Coen, the critical and commercial failure of which prompted Irvin Shapiro to suggest sequelising his debut feature. Although *The Evil Dead* ends abruptly, if not quite definitively, there was still the potential for the story to be continued in some fashion.

Collaborating with Scott Spiegel, Raimi initially envisaged *Evil Dead II* as having a medieval European setting, but the budget offered by legendary Italian film producer Dino DeLaurentiis ($3.6 million) was considered insufficient. It had been Stephen King, so instrumental in stoking up interest in *The Evil Dead*, who encouraged DeLaurentiis – whose sprawling production credits include Federico Fellini's *La Strada* (1954), Roger Vadim's *Barbarella* (1967), Michael Winner's *Death Wish* (1974) and David Lynch's *Blue Velvet* (1986) – to finance *Evil Dead II*, at this stage titled *Evil Dead II: Army of Darkness* (the title, along with the story, would be split across two sequels). Prior to *Evil Dead II* Raimi had been linked to an adaptation of *Thinner*, one of King's 'Richard Bachman' novels (the 1984 book would eventually be filmed by Tom Holland in 1996), while DeLaurentiis backed several King movies during this period: David Cronenberg's *The Dead Zone* (1984), Lewis Teague's *Cat's Eye* (1984), Mark L. Lester's *Firestarter* (1984), Daniel Attias' *Silver Bullet* (1985), King's directorial debut *Maximum Overdrive* (1986) and Tom McLoughlin's *Sometimes They Come Back* (1990).

Raimi and Spiegel were forced to scale down the screenplay and shift the medieval element to the end of the film (essentially one short sequence but this would blossom into an entire movie with *Army of Darkness*). Explains Bill Warren, 'They built the unusual, half-comic, half-serious approach into the script from the earliest drafts. It isn't a spoof, though some have regarded it as one; it's not making fun of any conventions of the horror genre. It doesn't contain overt, verbal jokes, and all the characters are essentially straight, not clownish. Instead, it treats straight elements for laughs, which is something more novel. It's the comic aspect of the movie that makes it unique – that, plus Raimi's astonishing style' (Warren 2000: 106-107).

So it was back to the cabin in the woods and back to Ash Williams battling demons. The film is frequently described as a rollercoaster ride, which, like *The Evil Dead*, it most certainly is. Kim Newman considers *Evil Dead II* as 'slapstick comedy which uses gore for gags' (Newman 1988/2011: 279), and this emphasis on humour over horror was crucial to the film's critical success, although its performance at the American box office was less satisfactory (the US theatrical returns were just under $6 million).

Evil Dead II

Evil Dead II ('the sequel to the ultimate experience in gruelling terror') opens in quite dramatic fashion with a microscopic remake of the earlier film, preceded by a collage featuring peculiar imagery and a voice-over narration which explains the history of the Book of the Dead:

> Legend has it that it was written by the Dark Ones... *Necronomicon Ex Mortis*... roughly translated, *Book of the Dead*. The book served as a passageway to evil worlds beyond. It was written long ago when the seas ran red with blood. It was this blood that was used to ink the book. In the year 1300 AD the book disappeared...

This time around rather than five young people travelling by car to a remote cabin location it's just two, Ash (Bruce Campbell) and girlfriend Linda (Denise Bixler). The cabin is now furnished with a piano, which Ash plays quite competently while Linda pirouettes like a ballerina. Ash discovers a tape recorder in the next room which contains a log entry from Professor Raymond Knowby (John Peaks), detailing in flashback his discovery of the Book of the Dead in the castle of Kandar. Along with his wife Henrietta (Lou Hancock), he returned to the cabin with the book. The professor's translation of the ancient text reveals that the book documents a 'spiritual presence, a thing of evil that roams the forests and the dark bowels of men's domain... It is through the recitation of the book's passages that this dark spirit is given licence to possess the living.'

Rather unwisely the professor decides to recite the very same destructive passages while Ash turns the pages of the flesh-bound book, and once these words are echoed from the tape recording the now-familiar Force hurtles its way through the woods towards the cabin and crashes through the bedroom window. Venturing into the dark forest in search of Linda, who has suddenly disappeared, he's confronted with her cackling, now-possessed presence but, as in the first film, he manages to decapitate her with a spade. Once he's buried her remains the growling Force smashes into the cabin and tears up to the terrified Ash (remarkably similar to the final shot of *The Evil Dead*). It is at this point that *Evil Dead II* ceases to remake *The Evil Dead* and takes on an identity all its own.

The Force spins Ash around on an incredible top-speed run amongst the tree-tops, ending only when Ash is dumped face down in a pool of muddy water. Emerging possessed like Linda, he is saved and returned to normality by the rising sun, which also has the power to cause the Force – the presence of the 'thing in the woods' is again signified by Raimi's 'Shaky-Cam' (though the shots are smoother and even more elegant this time), the guttural noises and swirling pockets of mist – to withdraw from whence it came. The bridge that serves as the mountain crossing to and from the cabin has been wrecked when Ash tries to make his escape, the framework wrenched upwards in an almost mocking gesture of demonic defiance.

In one of the film's best sequences, the Force pursues Ash as he drives back to the cabin, causing him to crash and be hurled through the rear window, over the seats and across the bonnet, before hurtling towards him as he approaches the cabin on foot. Bruce Campbell explains how this sequence was achieved:

> This Ram-o-Cam shot was particularly difficult. We tried to get this three times or so. [We used] a forty-five foot metal arm with an attachment for this little Eyemo camera. We all had to run with it, and when we got to the back of the car, we had to feed the arm through the car window. The rod was attached to a cart, but we had to lift it up to feed it through the window. Once we hit the trunk, and another time ran into the rear-view mirror. Sam wanted it to lift up; he didn't want it to go straight in. (Campbell in Warren 2000: 210)

The Force pursues him as he runs from door to door, room to room, only evading seizure when he finds a hiding place in the cellar (you get the impression that the Force could easily strip the cabin apart if it really wanted to completely possess Ash, suggesting that this might be just a terrifying game of cat-and-mouse). The film then cuts to an airstrip and introduces Annie (Sarah Berry) and her friend Ed (Richard Domeier); for a moment it appears that these characters have strayed in from another movie, but Annie is actually Professor Knowby's daughter and Ed a colleague of her father's. Annie has brought along with her additional pages of the book with the intention of completing the translation.

Back at the cabin Ash is tormented further. Linda's headless body rises from the grave and performs a dance before the laughing head re-attaches and detaches itself. She then emerges in the cabin, her head dropping into Ash's lap. He smashes it into the wall and the bookcase but still it continues to mock him. Ash destroys Linda's body with a chainsaw and does the same to her head after locking it in a vice in the tool shed.

More horrors are to follow: Ash's right hand begins to develop a life and mind of its own and, following an outrageous and very funny sequence in which the limb attacks him, Ash severs his hand with the chainsaw; the entire contents of the cabin suddenly come to life and it all becomes too much for the now one-handed, hysterical Ash.

Annie, Ed and two people they meet on the way, Jake (Dan Hicks) and Bobby Joe (Kassie Wesley), arrive at the cabin and, horrified by the blood and mess, suspect that Ash has murdered Annie's parents. While locked in the cellar Ash is confronted with Annie's possessed mother (played by Ted Raimi); the demons in this film, *Army of Darkness* and the subsequent television series *Ash vs. Evil Dead*, would be referred to as Deadites. Possessed Henrietta follows Ash when the others release him from the cellar and carnage unfolds: Ash stamps on the Deadite's head and one of her eyeballs flies out into Bobby Joe's mouth (one of the movie's finest gross-out moments); like Cheryl in the first film, Possessed Henrietta is shut in the cellar but mocks the others through the trapdoor; Ed becomes a Deadite and Ash despatches him with an axe; the spirit of Professor Knowby tells them to 'recite the passages, dispel the evil, save my soul, save your own lives'; Bobby Joe takes off into the woods and is attacked by the trees (there's no equivalent rape sequence, but the vines still give her a particularly rough time); Ash is briefly possessed again and comes for Annie, causing her to accidentally stab Jake; reverting back to normal, Ash straps the chainsaw to the stump of his right arm ('Groovy') and battles Possessed Henrietta with both the chainsaw and the shotgun, finally succeeding in blasting her to pieces; the ever-present Force finally reveals itself as a huge demon head (christened the 'Rotten Apple Head' by the film's crew); Annie is stabbed by Ash's disembodied hand while she's reciting the passages which will drive away the demons that have been unleashed, but Ash is pulled into a vortex (along with his car) and plummeted into what appears to be the Middle Ages. After shooting a winged Deadite out of the sky he is surrounded by knights in armour, who hail him as a hero.

Fig. 25 Annie, Jake, Ash and Bobbie Jo prepare to face the Deadites in Evil Dead II.

Unlike *The Evil Dead*, in which Ash is the only character to avoid possession, he succumbs in a most irreverent way in the sequel. Howard Berger, Robert Kurtzman and Gregory Nicotero – who would form the KNB EFX Group in 1988 – provided the film's special make-up effects, with Berger handling the make-up creations for Bruce Campbell, including the demonic 'Evil Ash' look, the hand and the mirror-twin:

> Bruce Campbell came into the shop so we could life cast him, then I produced a bunch of face positives, sculpted on top of those, cast and painted them all. Sam came in to look at Evil Ash's make-up... I just remember him going 'Yeah, maybe we can put more of a Witchiepoo [the wicked witch in the 1969 children's television series *H.R. Pufnstuf*] chin on it'. We had a day of test make-ups... all the make-ups were foam rubber back then, and you would do it all yourself, sculpting, breakdowns, sculptures, moulds, running your own foam, painting, etc... I put a PAX base all over the make-up, and then painted everything with rubber mask greasepaint and a stiple sponge. I used

> a Krylon pallette with purple and red inside the sockets to emphasise shadows and yellow for highlights, and painted all the cuts. The dentures I did the old Tom Savini way from his *Grand Illusions* book. I did a couple of sets, uppers and lowers. I took a mould of Bruce's teeth and built up the acrylic gums over that... so they were actually Bruce's teeth, but all crooked and twisted apart. We had Larry Odean do all the big white Sclerals contact lenses for us, obviously everyone was as blind as a bat wearing those. (Berger 2012, online)

Mark Shostrom collaborated with Berger, Kurtzman and Nicotero on the make-up effects - his respectable credits up to that point included Don Coscarelli's *The Beastmaster* (1982), David Cronenberg's *Videodrome* (1982) and Stuart Gordon's *From Beyond* (1986) – and recalls how conscious the team were of the need for an 'R' rating from the Motion Picture Association of America (MPAA), considering the 'X' which had been awarded to the first film:

> That whole rating thing was mostly to do with the blood and gore. Now there was a lot of gore that we shot that didn't get in the film because it was just too much. Sam was all for gory and he was all for funny, as long as we avoided an 'X' rating, and it basically came down to the red blood factor. I believe it ended up being unrated, which essentially can mean an 'X' to cinema owners. One of my favourite sequences was when Evil Ed gets the top of his head chopped off with an axe and he's still alive. We made a great puppet of him with half of his head gone, you could clearly see inside the skull, and the rest of his head was lying on the floor with the eyeball looking around, but that was just too much. I feel... that scene would have been so effective to show the whole thing and use red blood. None of us were really wild about using the multi-coloured blood, the green, the black and the brown... but it was the only way to avoid an 'X'.... If we'd showed everything in this film with real blood colour, it would certainly have been 'X' rated! Of course, when you have an 'X' rating, you're cutting out a huge chunk of your audience... which means a huge revenue loss. It was a question of: do you want your film to have a wide audience and make money by having an 'R' rating, or do you want to shoot whatever you want, then get an 'X' rating and have a small audience and make no money? There's no way a releasing company would ever allow that to happen. (Shostrom 2011, online)

Although the tone of *The Evil Dead* is far darker than the sequel, *Evil Dead II* is arguably the more satisfying of the two films in that its merging of wacky humour and gruesome, blood-spattered horror is more complete, more fully developed. The unexpected medieval setting of the finale would form the nucleus of the next film, *Army of Darkness*.

ARMY OF DARKNESS AND ASH VS. THE EVIL DEAD

In between *Evil Dead II* and *Army of Darkness* Sam Raimi directed *Darkman*, his first studio production, which combines elements of Michael Curtiz's *Doctor X* (1931) and *The Walking Dead* (1936) with the Phantom of the Opera and 1930s gangster films. In its comic book story the titular Darkman is Professor Peyton Westlake (Liam Neeson), whose experiments with synthetic flesh are disrupted when a ruthless and vengeful gangster, Durant (Larry Drake), sets fire to Westlake's laboratory, forcing the now-disfigured scientist to adopt a range of facial disguises to gain retribution. Something of a learning curve for Raimi, his experiences of working with a corporate entity like Universal – who gifted him a budget of $16 million – would reap rewards much later with his three mega-budget Spider-Man productions for Columbia/Sony: *Spider-Man* (2002), *Spider-Man 2* (2004) and *Spider-Man 3* (2007). *Darkman* was successful enough to spawn a brace of sequels executive produced by Raimi and directed by Bradford May, *Darkman II: The Return of Durant* (1995) and *Darkman III: Die Darkman Die* (1996).

Dino DeLaurentiis had already agreed to finance *Army of Darkness*, with Universal also a part of the deal. According to Bruce Campbell, the budget was initially set at $8 million but 'we figured we needed $11 million... the finished budget was around thirteen' (Campbell in Warren 2000: 144). Adds Raimi: '[*Army of Darkness*] is not so much a horror film as it is an adventure film – there's no gore. While there are still horrific effects, it's played more for comedy and adventure than to elicit a horrific reaction from the audience. The effects are slanted toward skeleton animation, and the magic and terror created by the Book of the Dead, vs the effects slanted toward the dissection of the human form. It's more fantasy rather than horror oriented. This one actually does have a story and more expanded characters' (Raimi in Warren 2000: 144/145).

While lacking the kinetic energy of the earlier films, *Army of Darkness* is an enjoyable romp that has fun with its medieval English setting (which makes for a welcome change from the bleak wintry woodland of *The Evil Dead* and *Evil Dead II*). It's very much a tribute to the stop-motion animation fantasies of Ray Harryhausen; in particular, *Army of Darkness* draws upon Nathan Juran's *The Seventh Voyage of Sinbad* (1958) and Don Chaffey's *Jason and the Argonauts* (1963) for inspiration as it resurrects those films' wonderfully weird and creepy warrior skeletons. Robert Kurtzman, Gregory Nicotero and Howard Berger supervised the film's special make-up effects, and one of the animators who worked on *Army of Darkness* was Pete Kleinow, formerly the pedal steel guitarist with legendary 1960s/1970s country rock band, the Flying Burrito Brothers.

The film opens with a quick re-cap of the story so far (Ash is revealed to work in a supermarket, while Bridget Fonda becomes the third actress to play Linda) but notably changes the ending from the previous film to have Ash taken prisoner after being whisked back in time to the year 1300. Once he escapes, Ash battles more Deadites, attaches a metal hand to his right stump in place of the chainsaw, encounters the Force yet again, is attacked in a windmill by miniatures of himself which emerge from his reflection in the shattered pieces of a mirror, suffers more torture when he grows an extra head on his right shoulder ('Evil Ash') before blasting it away with the shotgun (the head subsequently reanimates), Deadite skeletons led by Evil Ash form an army and create havoc until Ash leads Arthur (Marcus Gilbert) in an uprising; all the while Ash searches for the Necronomicon, which holds the key to his return to the twentieth century, only for the Deadites to follow him back to the S-Mart supermarket. The alternate ending, derived from Franklin J. Schaffner's *Planet of the Apes* (1967), has Ash travel too far into the future and be confronted with a post-apocalyptic landscape.

Following *Army of Darkness* there was no real enthusiasm from Sam Raimi, Rob Tapert or Bruce Campbell to have the series continue. As Tapert explained later, 'I don't know if there'll ever be a fourth *Evil Dead*, because they haven't made money. This is the truth. They've made money, but they haven't made *real* money, and it just doesn't pay for us to do it' (Tapert in Warren 2000: 177). Various video games (*The Evil Dead, Evil Dead: Hail to the King, Evil Dead: A Fistful of Boomstick, Evil Dead: Regeneration, Army of Darkness: Defense*) and comic books (*Army of Darkness: Shop Till You Drop Dead, Marvel Zombies vs. the Army of Darkness, Freddy vs. Jason vs. Ash, Freddy vs. Jason vs. Ash: The Nightmare Warriors*) filled the gap until 2015 when the world of the Deadites was resurrected in

Fig 26. A call to arms in Army of Darkness.

the form of a television series, *Ash vs. Evil Dead*. The show was essentially *Evil Dead 4* and it was Tapert's idea, following his involvement with the *Evil Dead* remake (see below), to develop the series with Raimi, his brother Ivan and Tom Spezialy. Ash is now 30 years older (much is made of his age and lack of sexual prowess) and is portrayed by Bruce Campbell as a lazy slob who resides at the Mossy Haven Trailer Park with a pet lizard for company. He drinks heavily, takes drugs, and works (in the loosest possible sense) at the Value Stop store for a sullen manager who views Ash as a freak. But he still has the Necronomicon in his possession, hidden in a trunk beneath a pile of men's magazines. A pair of co-workers, Pablo (Ray Santiago) and Kelly (Dana DeLorenzo), are reluctantly roped in to assist Ash with taking on the Deadites – it turns out that in the middle of a drug haze one of Ash's pick-ups quoted passages from the Book of the Dead which unleashed the demons once again, including the Force, which is now more destructive than ever. For financial and economic reasons New Zealand stands in for Michigan, USA (South Africa and Eastern Europe were also considered as shooting locations), Joseph LoDuca returned to compose the score, and Bridget Hoffman (the poster girl for *The Evil Dead*) provided the voice of the demonic doll which terrorises Ash in a warehouse. The enjoyable show ran for 30 episodes between October 2015 and April 2018 before its cancellation due to falling ratings.

Fig. 27 The return of Ash Williams in Ash vs. The Evil Dead.

EQUINOX

Before examining some of the films which *The Evil Dead* would inspire, it's worth spotlighting a low-budget horror movie from 1969 that shares some remarkable similarities with Sam Raimi's debut feature and makes for an intriguing precursor. However, there is no evidence to confirm that Raimi or any of his collaborators had seen this obscure oddity, and so the resemblance between the two films can be seen as a genuine and rather curious coincidence.

Written by Jack Woods and directed by Woods and an uncredited Dennis Muren (whose original conception was expanded upon by Woods and producer Jack H. Harris), *Equinox* is the story of a traumatised young man, David (Edward Connell), who is admitted to a psychiatric hospital after being discovered on the highway (he's been mowed down by a driverless car). In flashback it's revealed that he was one of a group of students on a picnic who decide to visit their college professor – played by the celebrated fantasy author Fritz Leiber (*Gather, Darkness!*, 1943, *Conjure Wife*, 1943) – but en-route are handed an ancient book of spells by a cave-dwelling old man. The professor steals the book and appears to have died following a fall only for his body to subsequently disappear. An unfriendly ranger (Woods himself), actually a demon in human form, attempts to rape David's girlfriend Susan (Barbara Hewitt) and the book is discovered to be a 'bible of evil', which can be used to call forth demons from another world; the professor has already succeeded in bringing these creatures into the present time. The stop-motion effects created by Jim Danforth and Dave Allen are fairly impressive (a winged demon, a green-skinned giant, a snake-like creature which consumes the professor's house) and the film remains distinctively weird and hallucinatory. In a typically inspired bit of programming, *Equinox* played on a double-bill with *The Evil Dead* at the Scala Cinema in August 1983.

EVIL DEAD REBOOTED

Fede Álvarez's *Evil Dead* (2013), which received its premiere at Austin's South By Southwest film festival in March 2013, is a re-interpretation of Sam Raimi's movie, an authorised remake in that it was produced by Raimi, Rob Tapert and Bruce Campbell. The basic ingredients remain the same but the mix is somewhat different and it leaves behind a rather sour aftertaste. That said, Álvarez's film (which he scripted in collaboration with Rodo Savagues) makes up in atmosphere what it lacks in scares and benefits from first-rate photography by Aaron Morton and production design by Robert Gillies.

In *Evil Dead* the five youngsters who visit a deserted cabin in the woods for the weekend are a messed-up bunch: Mia (Jane Levy) has a history of substance abuse, and her brother David (Shiloh Fernandez) is helping her go cold turkey. The others in the group, Eric (Lou Taylor Pucci), Olivia (Jessica Lucas) and Natalie (Elizabeth Blackmore), are barely on speaking terms. The cabin is in a sorry state; it's almost uninhabitable and the cellar is like something out of Tobe Hooper. 'You shouldn't have touched anything from that basement,' says Mia after David and Eric discover a shotgun and a book, which has been wrapped up and secured with barbed wire. 'Don't Say It, Don't Write It, Don't Hear It, They Open the Door to Him', are the words written on the inside cover, but Eric pays no heed to the warning. No sooner are the forbidden words spoken than the Force comes rushing towards the cabin, targeting Mia who is pursued through the damp woods, attacked by the vines, and 'raped' by the elongated tongue/vine of a female demon. Mia's dog is found with its head bashed in and David suspects that his sister may have been responsible; she soon shows visible signs of demonic possession, and the others are quickly infected and meet with unpleasant, splattery deaths.

Although the characters are as pitiless as they were in the original, and its bag of scare tricks too recognisable to have any meaningful effect, *Evil Dead* differs from the 1981 film in one important aspect. Having succeeded in releasing Mia from the spell and returning her to normal, David (this film's Ash Williams) is stabbed in the neck by the possessed Eric and then kills himself by blowing up the cabin. Now the Final Girl, Mia is forced to defend herself against the 'Abomination' (Randal Wilson) – who's been resurrected as the book demands that five souls be taken – and does so in a gutsy manner, tearing off her own hand to escape when it becomes trapped beneath a truck before slicing up the demon with a chainsaw. As the sun rises over the forest, the pages of the book begin to turn themselves over before the cover closes itself. Bruce Campbell makes an unbilled post-credits cameo and snippets of dialogue from *The Evil Dead* and *Evil Dead II* can be heard on the soundtrack.

An over-familiarity with the Deadite universe and the horrors it contains and transmits is one reason why *Evil Dead* is a far less satisfying film than the original. Technically, given the budget ($17 million) and high-end production values, the film is superior to the rough-and-ready original and Roger Murray's make-up effects and Bryan Shaw's pacy editing are both excellent. Yet the film too often relies on flimsy scares (barely glimpsed shadows hurrying across the screen accompanied by a loud 'whoosh' on the soundtrack, for example, or that old trick with the bathroom mirror), and it lacks the axis-tipping weirdness of Sam Raimi's film. Perhaps understanding the need to deliver something a little out of the ordinary rather than simply replay all of the events of the original, Álvarez opens his film with a pre-credits sequence in which a young girl (Phoenix Connolly), bloodied and bedraggled, is chained to a post in a foul dwelling surrounded by skinned animals and gore-covered tools. 'Don't be afraid,' speaks an old woman (Sian Davis) in a foreign tongue as she leafs through the pages of an arcane tome, the *Naturom Demonto*: 'Only the evil book can undo what the evil book has done.' The girl recognises one of her gathered abductors as her father (Jim McLarty), who explains to her that she was responsible for her mother's death. After dousing her with petrol and setting her alight, she transforms into a foul-mouthed demon. This event will serve as the backstory to the discovery of the book later in the film, as well as signposting the horrors which are to befall the main characters following their arrival at the cabin.

Elsewhere, the remake offers unsurprising variations on the original story. David and Eric's finding of the *Naturom Demonto* is a less creepy affair than first time around; rather than the trap door flinging itself open, the group are drawn to the cellar by Mia's dog and a smell 'like burnt hair' (the cellar is revealed to be the site of the 'cleansing' depicted at the beginning of the film). There's no tangible sense of something evil already at work here, no ominous mists or Shaky-Cam shots at this point.

The first 'appearance' of the Force is cross-cut with Eric foolishly reciting from the book, in spite of the warnings contained within and the tell-tale signs of its human-skin jacket and barbed-wire wrapping, and Mia suffering heroin withdrawal symptoms in the rain outside the cabin. The Force rushes towards Mia and there is a brief shot of a demonic face before Mia vomits. As she raises her head she glimpses what appears to be a young girl standing at a distance among the trees. This sequence suggests that there is a physical, human shape to the Force and that Mia has become the first to fall under its evil spell. By dispensing with the crazy dream-logic of the original and telegraphing its terrors to the audience, *Evil Dead* suffers not only because of its cold, serious approach to the subject but also because of its sheer lack of ingenuity. One such example is the equivalent tree rape, which has the trapped Mia confronted by the demonic girl, who spews thick black vines from her mouth that penetrate the upright Mia. It's a far less effective sequence than the original in that its combination of the sexual and the fantastic is orchestrated by a recognisable if not altogether human presence as opposed to the bewildering, invisible force behind the vines which attack Cheryl in Raimi's film. It's less spookily photographed, too, and takes place not in misty, unfathomable darkness but in stony grey daylight.

The transformations and demonic attacks are suitably violent and grotesque yet unmemorable; 'Evil Mia' is nowhere near as menacing as 'Evil Cheryl' and David/Ash doesn't know what to do with himself most of the time (Eric even calls him a coward at one point). Where the film does step up to the mark is in David's own transformation into a heroic, sacrificial figure; the scene in which he equips himself with chainsaw, shotgun, hypo and flashlight, accompanied by a succession of fast cuts and over-amplified sound effects, comes closest to capturing the spirit of *The Evil Dead* and *Evil Dead II*. His confrontation with 'Evil Mia' in the cellar, where he's aided by the barely alive Eric, isn't quite as impressive, but the sequence in which he tearfully buries what remains of his sister, who suddenly appears normal and leads to him hastily attempting to revive her after he's caused him to confront his guilt over his neglecting her for so long, is the film's strongest scene. Yet it seems somewhat out of place and unnecessary in an Evil Dead movie, and therein lies the inherent problem with the remake itself.

Fig. 28 Fede Álvarez's Evil Dead.

From the early 2000s onwards many of the horror movies which inspired *The Evil Dead* became the subject of glossier, bigger-budgeted, more professionally shot and acted remakes which invariably lack the intensity, brutal impact and political-social concerns of the originals, and it's fair to say that none of these films – among them Marcus Nispel's *The Texas Chainsaw Massacre* (2003), Zack Snyder's *Dawn of the Dead* (2004), Alexandre Aja's *The Hills Have Eyes* (2006) and Rob Zombie's *Halloween* (2007) – are anywhere near as invigorating as their models; some contain individual moments which work reasonably well but the films are ultimately inferior. Nispel's *The Texas Chainsaw Massacre* is unusual in that it is set in 1973 (the time period of the original) rather than the present day and gives Erin (Jessica Biel), the Marilyn Burns character, a moral purpose for survival. Snyder's *Dawn of the Dead*, bereft of the social commentary of the George Romero classic, revels in its use of nasty, fast-moving zombies as opposed to Romero's tragic, lumbering ghouls. The common thread which ties all of these works together is that they largely ignore the original movies and start from scratch; discussing Snyder's film, Kim Newman correctly remarks in *Nightmare Movies* that it aims for 'filmgoers who might be out of sympathy with the pacing, effects, politics, acting style, distribution pattern, certification, fashions or simply age of *Dawn of the Dead* (1978)' (Newman 1988/2011: 537).

Ghost House Pictures, the production company formed by Sam Raimi and Rob Tapert in 2002, has a history of manufacturing remakes and sequels: in addition to *Evil Dead*, their middling roster includes Takashi Shimizu's *The Grudge* (2004, based on his own Japanese horror from 2002, *Ju-on: The Grudge / Ju-on*), which was followed by two sequels, Shimizu's *The Grudge 2* (2006) and Toby Wilkins' *The Grudge 3* (2009), while the narrative of Nicolas Pesce's *The Grudge* (2019) exists concurrently with the events of all three films. Gil Kenan's *Poltergeist* (2015) fails to erase memories of Tobe Hooper's cosy yet still creepy Steven Spielberg-produced 1982 original, although despite the title Stephen Kay's *Boogeyman* (2004) bears no resemblance to Ulli Lommel's 'video nasty' from 1980.

BLOOD SIMPLE, *DEMONS*, *DEMONS 2*, *CABIN FEVER* AND *ANTICHRIST*

The earliest film to evoke the spirit and style of *The Evil Dead* was, coincidentally, the debut feature of two of Sam Raimi's associates, Joel and Ethan Coen. 1983's *Blood Simple* is the odd, moody, *noir*-ish tale of a Texas bar owner (Dan Hedaya) who hires a sweaty, untrustworthy private investigator (M. Emmet Walsh) to observe the movements of his wife (Frances McDormand, later to appear in *Darkman*), whom he believes is having an affair. Nothing is as it seems, the characters are off-kilter and strange, and there's even a scene which is reminiscent of one of the Force's POV shots as the camera hurtles at speed towards McDormand and Hedaya.

Produced and co-written by Dario Argento, Lamberto Bava's *Demons / Dèmoni* from 1985 and *Demons 2 / Dèmoni 2* (1986) delight in whacked-out, eye-popping horror. As intentionally illogical as *The Evil Dead*, *Demons* has a group of filmgoers (including Argento's eldest daughter, Fiore), invited to a special screening at a Berlin cinema, fall victim to a demonic plague that turns them into hideous, glowing eyed monsters. The plague is linked to the horror movie they have been invited to see, which literally crashes into reality when the first victim (who has scratched herself in the toilets on a venomous demon mask) staggers through the screen into the auditorium. Not quite as messy as its predecessor, *Demons 2* owes more to David Cronenberg's *Shivers / The Parasite Murders* and *Videodrome* as the tenants of an apartment block are transformed one by one into the same fanged demons ('Defend yourselves... defend yourselves!').

Eli Roth's *Cabin Fever* (2002) positions a group of over-sexed college kids (Rider Strong, Jordan Ladd, James DeBello, Cerina Vincent and Joey Kern) in a cabin in the woods and has them infected with a deadly disease which ravages their bodies. Lacking the intensity of *The Evil Dead* but nevertheless effectively capturing the horror of the situation as the friends lose their senses along with their body parts, the film was needlessly remade in 2016, scripted by Roth and Randy Pearlstein and directed by Travis Zariwny. It maximises the gory body horror but, apart from the introduction of a sinister yet attractively scar-faced female sheriff's deputy (Louise Linton), the film is dull and uninventive.

The Evil Dead's influence also seeps into the early, blood-drenched oeuvre of Peter Jackson (*Bad Taste*, 1987, *Braindead*, 1992) and Lars von Trier's remarkable psycho-drama *Antichrist* (2009), in which Willem Dafoe and Charlotte Gainsbourg engage in some graphic, almost unwatchable sexual violence in a cabin in the woods, as a rumination on grief and the nature of evil becomes nightmarish.

THE CABIN IN THE WOODS AND WITHER

The most entertaining, clever and self-aware of the *Evil Dead* variations is Drew Goddard's *The Cabin in the Woods* (2011). Goddard and his co-writer Joss Whedon mark our card early on that there is a high-level, high-tech and highly secretive, devilish experiment ongoing, and as the pieces fall into place it becomes increasingly clear to the audience that the five students on a country vacation are destined for a less than relaxing weekend. The cabin of the title is straight out of Raimi's classic: dark, unattractive, full of foreboding. The officials running the experiment allow the unwitting participants to make their own choices, but their destiny is in the hands of the 'directors' who effectively control the environment and the outcome and, in a sense, act as 'filmmakers' whose 'story' has a predetermined *dénouement*. The real filmmakers, Goddard and Whedon, are savvy enough to grasp that audiences are so familiar by now with the 'group-of-kids-in-jeopardy-in-a-log-cabin' scenario that this Rubik's Cube of a film playfully pokes fun at these conventions.

Atmospherically shot by Peter Deming, the group of friends explore the cellar (the guys at HQ have flicked a switch in the rigged cabin and opened the trapdoor for them) where they discover the personal belongings of a family who lived in the cabin in the early years of the twentieth century and suffered an awful fate as they each succumbed to demonic possession. Dana (Kristen Connolly) reads aloud from the daughter's diary but is stopped short by Marty (Fran Kranz), whose permanently stoned condition allows him to become more acutely aware than the others that there is more going on than meets the eye: 'I'm drawing a line in the fucking sand here, do not read the Latin,' he warns her to no avail.

Fig. 29 Drew Goddard's The Cabin in the Woods.

Somehow it doesn't really matter if the crumbling zombies she resurrects are real or part of the experiment, as at this point Goddard's film pays full and welcome homage to *The Evil Dead*. Juxtaposed with the gory mayhem that follows (the characters are genuinely expendable) we see the experiment 'directors' and their colleagues placing bets on which monster will participate in the 'story'; in this instance it's Zombies, but also up for selection are Vampires, Witches, the Mummy, a Redneck Torture Family and, best of all, Deadites and an Angry Molesting Tree. It's also revealed that similar experiments conducted around the world have recently failed, so the 'directors' are under pressure to deliver the goods.

Thanks to an explanatory cameo from Sigourney Weaver, this is all part of a series of sacrificial offerings to ancient gods; it's a noble, Lovecraftian concept that doesn't quite work as well as it ought to. The dazzling array of nightmare monstrosities which eventually overrun the complex – including what appears to be a Cenobite from Clive Barker's *Hellraiser* universe – allows the two survivors, Dana and Marty, to discover the awful truth: failure to satisfy the ancient ones who once ruled the Earth will lead to total destruction. In the final scene the cabin in the woods is sucked into the bowels of the earth.

Wither (2012), directed by Sonny Laguna and Tommy Wiklund, is an effective if minor Swedish shocker in which seven friends visit – yes, you guessed it – a cabin in the woods, mysteriously abandoned several years before. Soon after arriving for their get-together, the fragile Marie (Jessica Blomkvist) comes face to face with a creature of ancient legend and demonic possession is subsequently rife amongst the group (once possessed, human flesh becomes the order of the day). The backstory involves a family on a fishing trip who had visited the cabin two days earlier, with the wife and daughter falling victim to the demon in the cellar.

With the exception of the two leads, Albin (Patrik Almkvist) and Ida (Lisa Henni), the characters are too thinly sketched to elicit much sympathy, but the young cast deliver energetic performances and the film wears its Raimi and Romero influences well. Albin is also a Final Guy and, like Ash in the *Evil Dead* films, suffers enormous physical hardship. More, though, could have been made of the titular Wither (also played by Blomkvist), who is set free from the confines of the cellar but perishes in a terribly weak, rudimentary fashion.

Will the world of the Deadites ever be revisited? Can the spirits be called forth another time to wreak yet more havoc? Bruce Campbell recently considered his signature character to be 'retired', but Sam Raimi is more optimistic. After all, the remake concludes with the pages of the Book of the Dead flicking into life, and an alternate ending has Mia rescued only to show signs that she isn't quite as normal as she might appear to be. Since its first appearance in 1981, *The Evil Dead* has captivated fans and filmmakers alike with its energy, vitality, inventiveness, black humour and outrageous gore, and hopefully it will continue to do so for the next 40 years.

Bibliography

Baker, B. (2019) online interview http://www.bookofthedead.ws/website/interviews_betsy_baker.html

Barker, M., ed., (1984) *The Video Nasties: Freedom and Censorship in the Media*. London: Pluto Press

Becker, J. (n.d.) *The Evil Dead Journal* http://deadites.net/evil-dead-films/the-evil-dead/evil-dead-journal/12/

Becker, J. (2019) online interview http://www.bookofthedead.ws/website/interviews_josh_becker.html

Berger, H. (2012) online interview http://www.bookofthedead.ws/website/interviews_howard_berger.html

Butler, I. (1967) *The Horror Film*. London: Zwemmer

Carroll, N. (1990) *The Philosophy of Horror, or Paradoxes of the Heart*. New York: Routledge

Clover, C.J. (1992) *Men, Women and Chainsaws: Gender in the Modern Horror Film*. New Jersey: Princeton University Press

DeManincor, R. (2014) online interview http://www.bookofthedead.ws/website/interviews_richard_de_manincor_(hal_delrich).html

Dillard, R.H.W. (1976) *Horror Films*. New York: Monarch Press

Edwards, P. (1983) 'The Evil Dead'. *Starburst* (53), pp. 10

Egan, K. (2007) *Trash or Treasure? Censorship and the Changing Meanings of the Video Nasties*. Manchester: Manchester University Press

Fischer, D. (1985) 'Evil Dead'. *CineFan 3* (Winter / Spring 1984 / 1985), pp. 52-53

Freud, S. (1990) 'The Uncanny' (1919). *Art and Literature*. London: Penguin Books

Giles, J. (2018) *The Scala Cinema 1978-1993*. Surrey: FAB Press

Guttridge, C (2009) online interview http://www.bookofthedead.ws/website/interviews_cheryl_guttridge.html

Hardy, P., ed., (1985, revised 1993) *The Aurum Film Encyclopedia: Horror*. London: Aurum Press

Horsley, J. (1999) *The Blood Poets: A Cinema of Savagery 1958 – 1999 Vol. 1: American Chaos from 'Touch of Evil' to 'The Terminator'*. Maryland: Scarecrow Press.

Jaworzyn, S., ed., (1994) *Shock Xpress 2*. London: Titan Books

King, S. (1981) *Danse Macabre*. London: Futura

King, S. (1982) 'The Evil Dead'. *The Twilight Zone Magazine* (November 1982), pp. 20-21

Lucas, T. (2013) 'The Cabin in the Woods'. *Video Watchdog* (172), pp. 52-54

Martin, J. (1993, revised 1997) *The Seduction of the Gullible: The Curious History of the British 'Video Nasties' Phenomenon*. Nottingham: Procustes Press

Matthews, T.D. (1994) *Censored: The Story of Film Censorship in Britain*. London: Chatto & Windus

McCarty, J. (1990) *The Modern Horror Film*. New York: Citadel Press

Muir, J.K. (2004) *The Unseen Force: The Films of Sam Raimi*. New York: Applause.

Newman, K. (1982) 'The Evil Dead'. *Monthly Film Bulletin* (Vol. 49, No. 586), pp. 264

Newman, K. (1988, revised 2011) *Nightmare Movies*. London: Bloomsbury Publishing

Newman, K., ed., (1996) *The BFI Companion to Horror*. London: Cassell / The British Film Institute

Pierce, B (2011) online interview http://www.bookofthedead.ws/website/interviews_bart_pierce.html

Raimi, T. (2013) online interview http://www.bookofthedead.ws/website/interviews_ted_raimi.html

Russell, J. (2008) *Book of the Dead*. Surrey: FAB Press

Seyferth, T. (2019) online interview http://www.bookofthedead.ws/website/interviews_theresa_seyferth.html

Shostrom, M. (2011) online interview http://www.bookofthedead.ws/website/interviews_mark_shostrom.html

Spiegel, S. (2011) online interview http://www.bookofthedead.ws/website/interviews_scott_spiegel.html

Stoker, B. (1897, 1965 publication) *Dracula*. New York: Airmont Publishing

Sullivan, T. (2010) online interview http://www.bookofthedead.ws/website/interviews_tom_sullivan.html

Time Out review https://archive.is/20120629112310/http://www.timeout.com/film/reviews/64080/the_evil_dead.html

Towlson, J. (2018) 'Why *Night of the Living Dead* Was a Big-Bang Moment for Horror Movies' https://www.bfi.org.uk/news-opinion/news-bfi/features/night-living-dead-george-romero

Tudor, A. (1989) *Monsters and Mad Scientists: A Cultural History of the Horror Movie*. Oxford: Blackwell

Twitchell, J.B. (1985) *Dreadful Pleasures: An Anatomy of Modern Horror*. Oxford: Oxford University Press

Warren, B. (2000) *The Evil Dead Companion*. London: Titan Books

Williams, T. (2015) *The Cinema of George A. Romero: Knight of the Living Dead*. New York: Wallflower Press.

DEVIL'S ADVOCATES

"Auteur Publishing's new Devil's Advocates critiques on individual titles offer bracingly fresh perspectives from passionate writers. The series will perfectly complement the BFI archive volumes." Christopher Fowler, Independent on Sunday

CREEPSHOW – SIMON BROWN

Released in cinemas in 1982, Creepshow is typically regarded as a minor entry in both the film output of George A. Romero and the history of adaptations of the works of Stephen King. It is here reassessed by Simon Brown, who examines the making and release of the film and its legacy through a comic book adaptation and two sequels.

SHIVERS – LUKE ASPELL

Shivers (1975) was David Cronenberg's first commercial feature and his first horror film. Luke Aspell's analysis addresses all aspects of its production, including shot composition, lighting, cinematographic texture, sound, the use of stock music, editing, costume, makeup, optical work, the screenplay, the casting, and the direction of the actors.

THE TEXAS CHAIN SAW MASSACRE – JAMES ROSE

No-one who has ever seen The Texas Chain Saw Massacre (1974) is ever likely to forget the experience. An intense fever dream (or nightmare), it is remarkable for its sense of sustained threat. As well as providing a summary of the making of the film, James Rose discusses the extraordinary censorship history of the film in the UK and provides a detailed textual analysis of the film with particular reference to the concept of 'the Uncanny'.

www.ingramcontent.com/pod-product-compliance
Lightning Source LLC
Chambersburg PA
CBHW071413300426
44114CB00016B/2290